PRAISE FOR

Undefeated Woman

"Few of us know the story and struggles of those who come to the USA as refugees. This book documents the experiences of Desange and her family in the move from Congo to Uganda to Utah and the people who become part of their lives. It shares with those who read it both the external and internal debates that must be resolved in such a journey and provides readers with more understanding of, and empathy for, the refugee experience.

We learn much from *Undefeated Woman* about what gives meaning and hope to those who desire a better way of life and are willing to give so much of themselves to find fulfillment. This book is a great personal account of how to find meaning and determination."

—REV. FRANCE A. DAVIS, pastor emeritus of Calvary
Missionary Baptist Church, former member of Utah State
Board of Regents for the Utah System of Higher Education

"In *Undefeated Woman*, Desange Kuenihira takes us through her heartbreaking and raw journey from war-torn Democratic Republic of Congo to the suburbs of Salt Lake City, Utah. As she shares her innermost thoughts and feelings, we feel the strength of humankind, the bonds of family, and the power of education that can bring out the best in us. *Undefeated Woman* reminds us that the journey of our lives is indeed the destination."

—KRISTIN ANDRUS, philanthropist and advocate, organizer of
#SisterGoods Utah, board member, Ronald McDonald
House Charities of the Intermountain Area

Undefeated Woman

Desange Kuenihira

BrainTrust
I N K

The names and identifying characteristics of persons referenced in this book have been changed to protect their privacy.

BrainTrust Ink
Nashville, Tennessee
www.braintrustink.com

Distributed by River Grove Books

Design and composition by Greenleaf Book Group
Cover design by Greenleaf Book Group
Cover photograph by Courtney Gracie

Publisher's Cataloging-in-Publication data is available.

Print ISBN: 978-1-956072-06-8

eBook ISBN: 978-1-956072-07-5

First Edition

I dedicate this book to Mary Karungi and Florence Tibaleka, the women who have made me who I am today and who have been my motivation. You are the women who gave life to me, the women who raised me, nurtured me, fed me, taught me, and disciplined the Hell out of me when I got out of line (more often than not). I hope you know that I am here solely because you believed in me, you stood by me, and you prayed for me. You had all the reason to walk away, but you chose to stay.

CONTENTS

INTRODUCTION

IT ALL STARTED WITH HATRED. It took everything away from me: my home, my family, my friends, and my beautiful country. Oh hatred, what did I ever do to you?

Hatred is the worst thing in life. Even death is better. With death, you sleep peacefully. With hatred, you suffer.

My homeland is the Democratic Republic of Congo, where people killed each other for land, cows, and wealth. Innocent people died—were killed without mercy—because of hatred. Blood poured like waterfalls and people ran like prey chased by lions, desperate not to become the next meal. All of this death, all of this killing, it was all for wealth. But all that wealth, in the end, is meaningless. We all die and leave everything here. We come with nothing; we leave with nothing.

The Democratic Republic of Congo (DRC or Congo) is amazingly well-off and very large. Comparable in size to Western Europe, it is abundant in precious stones, gold, copper, coltan, and zinc. The people of Congo are not able to use or benefit from these resources because of the hatred caused by tribalism. Loyalty to tribe above all else stokes immense hatred, and those outside of Congo use that hatred to drive a wedge between African peoples to make it easier to take our wealth.

In 2006, the spine-chilling political conflict blockbuster *Blood Diamond,* set during the 1996–2001 Sierra Leone Civil War, increased public attention on the role diamonds mined in Africa play in funding violence. I saw this film and said to myself, people can live without precious stones; these stones often don't make someone feel fully satisfied. It's really simple: to avoid such grisly connections, don't accept precious stones.

Yet, that only solves one problem, for jewels are just one of our resources that is in high demand from all over the world. Hatred has blinded my fellow Congolese and Africans to the truth that people outside of Congo only want our country for its resources. They want our gold, copper, and tin. But more than anything, they want our coltan.

Coltan stands for columbite-tantalite, a mineral that can be refined into a heat-resistant powder crucial in the making of electronic circuitry used in today's most popular devices.[1]

While also found in Rwanda, Uganda, Burundi, Australia, Brazil, Canada, and China, the Democratic Republic of Congo has much of the world's coltan. As a primary exporter of coltan,[2] and with an abundance of other sought-after resources like gold, copper, tin, and precious stones, Congo is probably the most lucrative spot on the planet. With so much potential for wealth, why are the Congolese people in so much pain? Hatred and greed.

For decades, the tribes within my country have brutally fought each other. The money from mining helps fuel that fight, as mining

---

1   Kathy Feick, "Coltan," *Resources,* Earth Sciences Museum, University of Waterloo, accessed March 2022, https://uwaterloo.ca/earth-sciences-museum/resources/detailed-rocks-and-minerals-articles/coltan.

2   Oluwole Ojewale, "Child Miners: The Dark Side of the DRC's Coltan Wealth," *Premium Times,* October 18, 2021, https://www.premiumtimesng.com/news/top-news/490404-child-miners-the-dark-side-of-the-drcs-coltan-wealth.html.

proceeds are used to buy more weapons, continuing to fuel the awful twenty-year conflict happening within Congo that has taken the lives of six million people.[3, 4] And that constant inner conflict keeps the people of Congo from having a single voice that helps its people benefit from the riches within its land.

Hatred has taken all from Congo. Hatred, when will you stop? You have caused enough pain; you have spilled enough blood. Instead of helping a country grow and use resources wisely, hatred leaves all these innocent people crying day and night.

I am a refugee from Congo. I became a refugee because my own country—my own government—could not protect me. My leaders became greedy with Western money and only cared about their families instead of their country. They let their people suffer; they did not come together and fight for their people.

In Congo, people do not know who to work with. They tear each other down instead of lifting each other up. I have witnessed this not only in the conflict my family lived through and fled from, where tribes are killing each other daily because of their differences. Women are raped every day, children are killed, and men do not protect their own families. But even in the refugee camps, the places where we are supposed to be safe, people tear each other down.

Other countries have the power to help Congo, but it feels to me like they don't do much. Government officials seem to me like the

---

3   International Relations and Security Network, "Coltan and Conflict in the DRC," Relief Web, February 11, 2009, https://reliefweb.int/report/democratic-republic-congo/coltan-and-conflict-drc.

4   "Democratic Republic of the Congo," World Without Genocide, updated May 2020 by Zofsha Merchant, http://worldwithoutgenocide.org/genocides-and-conflicts/congo#:~:text=Since%201996%2C%20the%20Democratic%20Republic,bloodiest%20since%20World%20War%20IIconflicts/congo#:~:text=Since%201996%2C%20the%20Democratic%20Republic,bloodiest%20since%20World%20War%20II.

most secretive people ever, hiding what they do and rarely being honest. They do not want people to know the truth. I am so tired of seeing innocent people die every day.

I wonder how my life would have turned out if I still lived in my home country. Maybe I could have made a difference. I am not saying I can't make a change now; I can and I will. That's why I do the work I do: spread awareness of the pain my people face and empower women and children with opportunities for education and the skills to shape their own futures.

But sometimes I just feel powerless. It puts me in tears knowing that my leaders haven't changed, not knowing if the rest of the world cares, watching others go to Congo and take what belongs to my people.

I believe there comes a time when you get tired of seeing your own people die. There comes a time in life when you say *enough is enough*. There comes a time when you understand your country's worth and your own.

· · ·

I wish I had a chance to grow up in the country where my roots began. But that is not how my journey has been written.

In Congo, and later in the refugee camp in Uganda, I knew education was my only way out of poverty. But education seemed like a distant, unattainable dream. I saw myself getting married when someone else decided I should, probably when still quite young, and having kids I could not provide for. From there, the cycle would just keep repeating itself. Whenever I thought about this future, I cried.

The norms of my culture considered me meaningless because I was just a girl. In my culture, a marriage is recognized when cows are given to the bride's father as a dowry. That dowry should be a recognition that the family raised a beautiful woman who brings much to her new family. Instead, too many fathers see that dowry as just a source of income. Too many men see the dowry as buying a wife. Too few understand that you cannot buy a human being.

I felt unvalued by my people, my family, and my friends. I didn't even see my own value. This is what happens when you get called a meaningless girl by people who are supposed to love you. The person in charge of caring for me first called me a meaningless girl when I was just about six or seven years old. My fellow refugees and the children I went to school with called me a meaningless girl throughout childhood, as did the young teens I sang with in a church choir. None of them understood me. They saw someone with strength inside, strength against hatred, strength they feared. Strength they tried to break with ugly words.

For too long, I listened to those hateful words, and I could do nothing about them. I believed them. And that sucked all the good out of me. I felt that I was never seen. Listening to other people broke me and pushed me deep into my own world—the darkest place I have ever been.

I was scared of the condition I was in with so many things ruined in my head. I've never felt more helpless, and I hope I will never go back to that place where I felt like I would never be someone. I was always angry and I did not love myself. I blamed myself for everything—everyone was perfect except me. I couldn't believe in myself. I broke myself down and held myself back. The hate I had for myself was greater than the hate I had for those who wronged me.

I was an unhappy person; I was the meanest person. All I did was ruin people's moods. I showed aggression toward kids and fought with my elders. I disrespected people because I wanted them to see something good in me, but I knew they didn't.

They saw something else: a monster girl, meaningless, living a life with no purpose. I wanted to prove something to the world, but I was wasting my time. How can the world see something in me when I could not even see it myself? I wanted people to value me, but I did not value myself. I had expectations of the world. But I couldn't take on the world until I believed in my worth and found my voice.

This is my story, my journey. From conflict to safety. From poverty to opportunity. And most of all, from meaningless girl to a confident woman. A woman with a voice. A woman ready to speak, undefeated.

I have not let my past define me; instead, it has been my motivation. I refuse to be a victim to what happened to me. I choose to be a warrior. The best thing I have ever done for myself was to take the journey to discover who I am. When I understood who I was, I found an unDEfeated woman.

"Life will never knock you down unless you let it."

—*Desange Kuenihira,*

Once a meaningless girl, today unDEfeated woman.

unDEfeated

www.speakunDEfeated.org

1

FLIGHT AND SOME SALVATION

YOU COULD SAY MY STORY BEGINS when I was just two years old when my siblings and I fled our home in the middle of the night, fearing for our lives. But my story actually starts years before.

In 1998, tensions still simmered after the First Congo War had gone dormant the year before. Soon, those tensions escalated and the Second Congo War erupted. In the midst of that war, the ruling government chose to make a new province, Ituri, in the part of eastern Congo where we lived. The Congo leaders' choices of who governed Ituri plus the violent presence of militia groups backed by factions from nearby countries added fuel to the conflict between the Hema and Lendu, the two main, and very different, tribes in the region. They both make their living from the land, but in ways that feel incompatible to many—Hema are herdsmen that graze cattle; Lendu farm the land. And each have viciously attacked the other, at times massacring entire villages, as the region has been torn apart by war. Many innocent people from both sides and many other tribes were caught in the middle.

My five siblings and I were stuck in the middle, too. Not just by living in the middle of a region plagued by violence, but by not being solely of one tribe. Intermarriages between tribes have always happened, but few in our culture approved of such marriages. And the more conflict raged, the more hatred grew, the more our intertribal faces looked to those around us not as the faces of children, but as the faces of betrayal and of danger.

We lived in a village where my father's father had a large herd of cows. For many tribes across Africa, cows are wealth, as the money from the sale of one cow could feed a family for about six months. The herd was as important to protect as a bank account would be to a Westerner. As long as things were peaceful, my father's family tolerated the presence of his wife and children.

In 2003, as the war drew near our village, the adults in the family felt they had to stay and protect their homes and their herd but sent the grandchildren to the town of Bunia to live with my uncle, where they hoped we would be safe. But soon news reached Bunia that people throughout the region had been slaughtered. The war was coming closer, and fearing the approaching violence, my eldest brother, Badulu, decided we should flee Bunia in the middle of the night to Uganda.

Badulu was only eighteen. Alfred, the next oldest, just sixteen. Together, they helped me and my siblings run. My sister Zawadi was four, I was two, my brother Tusiime was one, and my little sister, Irini, was just a tiny infant. It was a difficult journey. It was chaos. On foot over the green hills and grasslands, we followed the path of other terrified refugees the roughly twenty miles from Bunia to Lake Albert, the crossing to the Ugandan border.

We ran as best we could on the dirt roads during the night and hid in what cover we could find during the day, which meant we rarely slept. Often, we lay under sparse bushes, our brothers' hands over our mouths so we wouldn't cry, making ourselves as still as possible so that we didn't rustle the grass and give ourselves away. Occasionally, we'd get lucky and find a cave.

We did not have food to eat. Sometimes we foraged for food in the gardens we passed. We drank what little water we could find from small streams or containers outside of people's homes, resorting to sipping cow urine from puddles when we were desperate with thirst. How my brothers fed baby Irini, who didn't yet eat solid food, I don't know. I remember she cried so much. With all of us little ones, we had to move slowly, and so it took us about three weeks to get to the shore of Lake Albert. From there, we packed into small, overcrowded fishing boats that took us across the lake. UN reports say the crossings across Lake Albert often take refugee boats ten hours to reach the other side since they are overloaded and can easily tip, dangerous since most Congolese do not know how to swim.[5] I don't know how long it took us, but by the time we reached the Ugandan border, like many refugees, we could barely walk. It took us nearly a week to physically recover.

. . .

On the Ugandan shore, aid workers fed us, helped us get clean, and let us rest while we waited our turn to be taken to Kyaka II, the refugee camp in Uganda most Congolese from our region were sent to at the time. After three days, we piled into buses that drove us a few hours until we finally reached the refugee camp.

---

5   Walter Kigali and Catherine Wachiaya, "Refugees Flee Fresh Fighting in Congo to Uganda," *UNHCR|USA* (blog), February 13, 2018, https://www.unhcr.org/news/stories/2018/2/5a81779e4/refugees-flee-fresh-fighting-congo-uganda.html.

Badulu needed to find some adult to care for us children because he and Alfred were considered adults and wanted to go find work and make a living in Uganda. A friend of Badulu told us that he had seen Tibasima, a woman from a village near our father's who knew of and respected my father and grandfather and was there without children of her own to feed. Hoping she would be willing to care for us, we began our search for her. At that time there were over a thousand people in the camp (in a year, that number grew to over six thousand),[6] and so it took us an entire week to find her. The moment we did was a moment of sheer joy for us all. She took us to the small home that the United Nations High Commissioner for Refugees (UNHCR), a relief organization, had given her to live. She told us what had happened and that a lot of people were killed back where we escaped from.

Many think of tent cities when they think of refugee camps, but Kyaka II was more like a village. The refugee settlements in Uganda were run according to the government's philosophy of self-reliance, where refugees were given a small plot of land on which to build a shelter and grow their own food with access to government-provided education and health support.[7] In the Kyegegwa District of Uganda, Kyaka II sits on about eighty kilometers of rolling hills with small streams of water running through. Divided into zones, the settlements in the camp are collections of small homes with about four rooms and structures for schools, a health center, a police building, and a camp

---

6   Sarah Dryden-Peterson, "The Present Is Local, the Future Is Global? Reconciling Current and Future Livelihood Strategies in the Education of Congolese Refugees in Uganda," *Refugee Survey Quarterly*, 25, no. 2 (2006): 81–92. https://doi.org/10.1093/rsq/hdi0127.

7   "Self-Reliance Strategy (1999–2003) for Refugee Hosting Areas in Moyo, Arua, and Adjumani Districts, Uganda," Report of the Mid-term Review by Government of Uganda and UNHCR, April 2004, RLSS Mission Report 2004/03, https://www.unhcr.org/41c6a4fc4.pdf.

office.[8] There were even a few gathering places, including a café, at the center portion of the camp that we called "town."

How the homes and buildings were constructed depended on when they were built. The homes at our time in our zone were made from a framework of small tree branches, about the size around of a man's arm, lashed together and filled with mud made from the local red earth. Some roofs were made of metal, others canvas covered with branches to keep the fabric from blowing off. The floors were nearly always hard-packed bare earth, swept clean. There was enough space around the homes for families to tend small sustenance gardens.

There was no electricity, no plumbing. Our toilets were outhouses, which multiple families often shared. We fueled our small stoves with charcoal we had to buy. We used jerry cans—bright yellow plastic containers originally filled with cooking oil, then cleaned out and repurposed for water storage—to carry water from water stations, wells, and springs and washed our clothes in the not-so-clean streams.

We younger children lived with Tibasima, who shared with us what provisions she received from the camp, and we helped with the chores and tended the garden. Badulu and Alfred lived away from the camp, wherever they could find work, sending money to Tibasima for food for us when they could.

We lived in the refugee camp until I was about eleven years old. Life was hard. There was not enough to eat, people could be unkind, and our future was so uncertain. But it was interesting, and sometimes

---

8   MapAction, REACH, UNHCR, "Facilities Map—Kyaka II Settlement—Kyegegwa District—Uganda, 24 October 2018," ReliefWeb, October 24, 2018, https://reliefweb.int/map/uganda/facilities-map-kyaka-ii-settlement-kyegegwa-district-uganda-24-october-2018.

even fun. There was a lot of drama that distracted us from feeling hungry or thinking about the situation we were in. It seemed like something happened or people fought almost every day.

. . .

At the camp, the first man we met was named Amatoke. He worked with a refugee organization and helped us in many ways, like sometimes buying us food. He was a man who treated everyone the same—with respect. He and Tibasima developed a relationship, and soon we all lived together at the camp, and for part of the time, years later, we lived in Kampala. Amatoke became like a father to us. When we were leaving for America, he came to the airport to say goodbye. We still talk to him and help him when we can.

He was a fun guy to live with—very supportive and funny. Sometimes he would even go to church with us to pray. He taught us many things, like how to cook. Surrounded by many cultures, he cooked with ingredients we weren't familiar with.

There was one thing he hated: disobedience. If he told you to do something and you didn't do it, then you weren't friends for a while. One time he told Tusiime, who was about five years old at the time, to do the dishes. Tusiime avoided the chore all day. Amatoke found out that night while changing, and with just a towel wrapped around his waist, chased Tusiime and warned him, "I'm going to beat you for disobeying me." They ran in circles around the house, Tusiime keeping out of reach, the rest of us laughing because it was such a funny sight. Finally, Tusiime ran out the door toward town. Amatoke skidded to a stop. He wasn't about to run out of the house in just a towel! Mostly, however, if we did something bad, he would simply tell us, "You need to change here and here." We listened to him and learned from him and accepted him for who he was.

He wasn't perfect. He ignored at first how Tibasima treated us, and later copied some of her ways. Although Amatoke was an important part of my life in Uganda, because he was away so much, he wasn't at the camp during the big events I'm sharing in this book. So, I choose to remember the good side of him, because that is what made an impression on me.

He fought for us in many ways. At one point, he lost his job because of his relationship with Tibasima, but no matter the cost, he chose to help us anyway. He got a new job in Kampala that required him to travel for weeks and sometimes even months at a time. He usually came home with money and bought food for us. Later, when we lived in Kampala, he wanted us to go to school, but did not have any money to pay for it.

Often, I asked myself, "Why is he doing all of these things for us? Who are we to him? Are we better than all those other refugees?" No, we are not better than anyone—I know I am no more perfect or beautiful than anyone else—Amatoke's kindness was God's mercy on us. God heard our prayers and answered them. God will really surprise you in many ways.

This man taught me that I can do anything if I am willing to sacrifice myself and make hard decisions. In this world, it is hard to find true love and true friends, but Amatoke knew how to love and showed me what it looked like. He taught me that family is not always blood. Family can be people who want to be in your life and want you to be in theirs.

Saying goodbye to Amatoke was one of the hardest things I had to do. I had to learn that the right people will always stay in your life and will always be there and support you, fight for you, and see you through until their time to help you is done.

2

MEANINGLESS GIRL

AFTER TWO WEEKS IN THE REFUGEE CAMP, we started school. None of the other kids wanted to play with us. We may have left the war behind, but the hatred between tribes and the prejudice nearly everyone had against marriages between tribes followed us to the refugee camp. People still hated each other, and so life was hard.

It was hard living in an environment where people didn't like you and made it known. Not only were we hated, but people who liked us or talked to us or became friends with us were hated, too. However, at least they were truthful to who they were. They had honesty, which I think is the best thing you can ever offer someone, because then at least you know where you stand.

At first, I tried to please people so that I would be liked and fit in. I wanted to be seen as a normal human being, not as a murderer, which is what many people saw when they saw the face of a tribe different than theirs.

But nothing I did made anything change. I didn't understand it then, but I know now that pleasing people was not going to change anything in their minds or their hearts about other tribes or kids like me from more than one tribe. Only they could change their own perspective.

Trying to please people set me up for them to use me. They acted like a greedy stomach that instead of saying thank you after a meal always wanted more. And so soon, about as young as four years old, I stopped trying to please people, because I realized that people hated me no matter what I did. Being hated was my everyday life, and I got used to it.

I remember other kids beating us up at school as early as when I was only three years old. We were an easy target since we didn't have a father's protection or a mother's love. We needed someone to defend us and fight for us. That someone became me.

Kids picked on my sister Irini a lot because she was so small and frail. And I did not like it. Whoever touched her had to hear from me. It did not matter who touched her, I would fight anyone. Soon, kids were scared of me. If they saw me coming, they would run away. This made me feel safe. It made me feel like my voice was heard. Being the monster girl made me feel hopeful, powerful, and strong.

I didn't even respect my elders. If people did not see value in me, in my mind, then they did not deserve my respect. Especially when they called me a meaningless girl.

Tibasima was the first person I remember calling me that. I was about six or seven, cooking corn into porridge in a little charcoal stove set up between our house and our small garden of corn. Tibasima told me to stir in the milk. I went into our house and grabbed the yogurt she meant for me to use and poured the entire container's worth into the pot.

She was agitated that day. Something, I don't know what, already had her upset. She asked me if I put all of the yogurt in, and I said yes.

"Meaningless girl!" Tibasima spat out and slapped me across the face.

The slap stung, but I wasn't about to let her see she'd hurt me. I grabbed a jerry can and told her I was going to fetch water. But really, I found a tree out of sight from Tibasima and our neighbors, dropped the can, and climbed high until the leaves hid me from view. And I cried.

Looking back, I think in that moment she just took out her stress on me, but at the time I was too little to understand that. Whatever the reason she had for being cruel, I could no longer respect her. Once any elder yelled at me or called me names, I no longer trusted them.

One time, also when I was about six years old, I was fetching water when a woman carrying a child on her back approached me. She had not brought anything to use to get water from the water station. After I finished fetching my water, I grabbed everything that I had come with and started walking up the hill.

She stared at me a moment, then said, "Can you please help me out?"

I looked back briefly, then kept going with no response. This woman had yelled at me before. Why should I help her?

I got to the top of the hill, turned, and stared back at her for about a minute. Her baby started crying. The sun was going down, and as I stared at her, the sun hit me in the face.

She said, "I know deep down a beautiful heart is in you. I know that most people do not see good in you. You have been our topic of conversation for a while now. Our children fear you. Even other older people are scared of you."

"Why are people scared of me? Why do you all talk about me?" I asked.

"The little kids fear you because you beat them up. The older ones . . . I am not sure why."

"Are you scared of me?"

"Yes, I am."

"Why? I am just a girl who is trying to survive. Do you think people treat me and my siblings well?"

"No."

I had so many more questions, but I did not want to ask them of her. I knew everyone had a different opinion of me. At the end of the day, it did not matter. I walked back down the hill and handed her the cup I used to fetch water.

She said, "Thank you so much," smiling at me. I did not smile back—I knew she said all of that to just get the cup so she could fetch water.

As I walked back home carrying jugs of water on my head and in my hands, I thought about our conversation. She had said she knew deep down I had a beautiful heart. Part of me did not believe it, but another part of me wanted to know if some people really did see good in me despite everyone else in camp deciding I was bad.

About twenty minutes after I got home, she returned the cup. As I watched her walk away through the gardens bordering our homes, I washed the cup really well, afraid she'd put voodoo in it to curse me. I truly have never forgotten her conversation with me because, even though I did not believe anything from her mouth, she was the first person to tell me there was a beautiful heart inside of me.

• • •

Growing up, I was abused in many ways—physically, verbally, and sexually. Some incidents I still can't talk about. But in particular, two brothers from the same family sexually abused me when I was about six or seven years old on more than one occasion. I am not sure if they planned it.

Being sexually abused as a kid took a lot from me. I lost myself at a very young age. I couldn't get help—I did not have trusted adults to turn to. I couldn't go to Tibasima and tell her. I remember struggling to try to see if there was a way, but all I could think was that if I told Tibasima, she would most likely beat me, so I kept it to myself. I pretended like nothing ever happened; I did not show anything.

The first time I was sexually abused, I was six years old. It was late in the afternoon, and I was going to fetch water at a station in a little valley surrounded by hills. It was a beautiful day, but the sun was setting, and I started to get chilly as I was only wearing a red dress that came to my knees.

I started filling the two jerry cans I had with water. A tall young man, probably in his twenties, came to the water station and got close to me. He smiled and said hi. I said hi back. Then he asked, "Why do people think you're a monster?"

By this time, I did not like talking to people. And I really did not like people coming to me and telling me what others were saying about me, because it was never good. "Do you see me worried about it?" I said. "I have no problem with people calling me a monster. That is their problem."

I finished fetching my water and started heading up the hill. He told me to wait so we could go together.

"Why should I wait for you?" I said. "Did I come with you?"

I could tell the way I was talking back to him was making him mad. I started getting scared and began walking fast. He started saying bad words to me and yelling at me, "That's why people do not like you! You are just mean to people for no reason!"

I did not respond and kept walking fast. I was afraid he might do something to me, and so I rushed to get to the top of the hill. That way, if anything did happen, people would be able to hear me scream and help me.

I made it to the top of the hill and saw him running up the hill after me with his water. I was tired after running with full jerry cans of water and decided it was safe to take a break and catch my breath, thinking nothing could happen up there where people could hear and see me.

He caught up to me. "So you thought you were fast?" he taunted me.

"Can you go? Since you seem to be the King of Fast," I said.

He grabbed my breast (I was very young when I began to develop and my breasts were already budding at that age), then said, "I can do anything I want to you."

I backed up, grabbed a nearby stick and told him to go away. I picked up my water and started walking away from him, but he stuck his foot under my foot and tripped me.

I was scared like I'd never been before. Flashes of heat and chills shot through my body, I was so scared. He grabbed me and laid me down and started pulling my dress up. I screamed for help.

"You think you are the toughest girl," he said. "You think, 'Well I am tougher than they are.' I am going to teach you a lesson today."

He started pulling off my underwear, and something came over me. I felt so powerful. As he started undoing his pants, I bit his cheeks, and then I kicked him where it hurt. He let go of me, and I threw dirt in his eyes. Then I quickly ran into a nearby garden of corn to hide.

I heard him screaming; I heard him searching for me. I was so scared, but I did not run to get help. I just hid. I knew no one would believe me; they would believe his story over mine. I stayed in the garden crying for about thirty minutes. After I heard other people coming to fetch water, I got out, cleaned myself off, and went home.

I did not say anything to my siblings or Tibasima. I kept quiet. This was the first time I ever felt helpless over the fate of my body. The only good thought I had was that I was glad he did not rape me. I sat on the bed, trembling with anxiety's rattle and hum. The sky was bleak, with charcoal clouds that seemed to mirror my soul. The fog of depression, all too familiar to me at even that young age, had rolled in, and I was weary of the struggle. I couldn't sleep, and I cried the whole night. I did not make any noise, tears just silently poured out of me.

Verbal attacks kept coming my way. I was still so young, only about seven years old, when women in the village showed what they thought of me again.

I went to fetch water and found a bunch of kids crowding the water station, all with their cups out. Even at that age, I was tired of people making my life harder, and that day, I just couldn't wait my turn. I said, "Everyone move. I'm fetching water."

The other kids scattered, and I got the water I needed. Kids came back when I was done, and being seven, I got a silly idea. I thought it would be fun to see if I could jump all the way over another little girl. So I put my water down and leap-frogged over her.

Her mother saw this and was so angry. She came over and started yelling at me. She threatened to beat me if I ever did anything like that again. She said, "Who do you think you are?"

"Mind your own business," I shot back. "I'm taking my water home, and I'm going to leave in one piece."

The woman looked at me and said, "That's why nobody likes you. The way you act, that's why people hate you." She said, "You're so meaningless. There's no point to you. You are nothing here."

I ignored her, got my water, and left. But that night, it all hit me. Tibasima slapped me if I misunderstood her and called me meaningless girl. A man chased me and assaulted me, saying he could do what he wanted to my very young body. The women of the village said I was meaningless, too. It felt like I couldn't escape abuse. I wasn't wrong.

The second sexual abuse incident happened soon after, when I was still only about seven. I had left school early because I was not feeling well. I was wearing the green dress that was my uniform, and my stomach felt just as green.

I took the fast way home on small roads, dirty with car exhaust, that cut through the countryside that lay between the school and our homes. The older brother of the first young man who assaulted me rode slowly by on his bike. We said hi to each other, and he asked me why I was not at school. I explained I wasn't feeling well, and he offered me a ride on his bike. I refused.

"You know, you are beautiful," he said.

"Okay," I said and kept walking. I always found it disgusting when men told me I would be so beautiful when I grew up. I knew what that meant, the one thing they were thinking about. Even that young, I knew.

"Come here," he said.

I said no and started running, crying and screaming.

He chased after me. Since he was on his bike, he caught up to me easily. He grabbed my backpack and yanked it backward. I fell on my back, and it knocked the wind out of me. I tried to get up, and he pushed me back down to the ground. Then, he started to undo his pants.

I thought, *He is going through with this.* I was scared, so very scared, with so many thoughts and emotions coursing through my brain. Why would this man want to attack a young girl like me? Why did I have to be sick? I had a flash of anger with myself, thinking this wouldn't have happened if I had been healthy and in school instead of falling ill and walking home early, alone. I couldn't think how to get away; I felt hopeless. And I felt so tired. I did not feel any power within me.

I remember him calling me "meat of the week." He said a lot of things in his language that I could not understand. He held my hand on my chest and tried to take my dress off. Maybe it was the pressure of him pushing my hand into me, maybe it was fear, maybe it was just being sick, but my stomach rebelled. First, I farted and he stopped for a moment to hold his nose. Then I felt nauseous. He still held his nose with one hand and me against the ground with the other, but I managed to push myself up and vomit all over him. He let go, and I ran to the main road as he sat there mumbling, trying to clean the vomit off himself.

My world was lonely; I felt unsafe everywhere I went. At night I had to cover myself with at least three blankets to feel safe. It was my way of coping with the pain and fear. I started having bad dreams of being chased by that man. I blamed myself—I believed that I was bad and that maybe if I had talked to him nicely when he said I was beautiful, the assault would not have happened.

The fog of my depression formed a dense wall, hedging me into isolation. Most days, it seemed nobody, not even God, could break through. But this pain was nothing new. I couldn't remember a time when depression's waves didn't roll through me. For years, then and later, I grew accustomed to smiling and saying nothing was wrong, I was just tired, while I did my best to do whatever I had to do while my chest burned and my body felt like lead. It was exhausting—wrestling to be whole, never shaking the bone-deep loneliness. There's an excruciating physicality to mental illness that's rarely acknowledged.

I allowed these assaults to silently choke years out of my life. I was broken in every area of my life. I walked around with a fight inside me. I felt completely lost and helpless. Everything I did was in an attempt to force my feelings deep down and forget what had happened to me.

I could not break the chains of depression. Life spun out of control. I felt as though I had been left alone to deal with the mental, physical, and emotional mess that was my life after these assaults on my body and my heart. It felt like I was in a deep hole. It felt like I was in Hell.

Some of the people who tried to hurt me were very dear to me. They were the people that I truly trusted and thought would protect me. I lost trust in every person I knew. I did not even trust myself. I pushed friends and family away. I was afraid I would end up alone. The fear was unbearable at times. Shame covered me and I didn't understand that God would still love me no matter what my past looked like.

It took me a very long time before I found myself. My recovery was long, ugly, and painful. I had to dive deep inward to heal the anger, sadness, and even rage that came from the abuse.

I've been hurt by a lot of men. And so I hated men—all men—for the longest time. I viewed them all as the same, instead of recognizing that each individual person can be different. I avoided dating completely until very recently. *Who are you?* I would think of any man that showed interest in me. *Why should I give you my time?* Even now that I've dipped a cautious toe into the dating pool, I'm still overly aware of my surroundings. I'm always on edge.

The abuse inflicted on me helped me be an independent woman. I now sometimes think, what human hasn't been hurt by another human? I'm not trying to downplay my own trauma. It just doesn't hold the emotional charge it once did because I've processed the pain. Or have I?

But finding myself only happened recently. Then, at the refugee camp, I was still a young girl. And because of all of these emotional, physical, and sexual assaults, I felt worthless. I lost even the little confidence I had in myself. I just started thinking maybe being *worthless* and *meaningless* should be my middle names.

3

THE TURMOIL AROUND ME

LESS THAN A YEAR LATER, my siblings and I were walking home from school one day, trudging through mud leftover from the day's rain. I wasn't talking as much as I usually did to my siblings. It felt like something was off. There was tension in the air.

As we passed through town, we saw two white cars in the road covered in green leaves, like when a big storm with heavy winds showers leaves on everything around. But there was more damage—someone had slashed the tires. The two cars were ruined. The small market by the road was empty. Throughout the town, the small businesses were closed. Lots of people were standing around outside, some wearing black T-shirts, nearly all seemed so angry.

My siblings and I wondered what was going on, but we didn't dare ask anyone. We just walked straight home. When we got home, we asked Tibasima what was happening in the town center. She told us protesters, tired of being hungry because the refugee office wouldn't give us food, decided it was time to get food by force. They had swarmed the car of the kamandati, a Ugandan that was the head officer of the refugee camp, as he passed through the town center. The protestors had hit the kamandati's car with trees and stabbed its tires.

Tibasima told us the kamandati had to escape. He ran through the gardens between homes, scared for his life as people chased him. The kamandati did not like Tibasima at all, and the whole camp knew it. He always called her bad names, both in private and in front of everyone. But it wasn't just Tibasima; the kamandati had a poor relationship with nearly all the people in the camp. He hit refugees; it didn't matter if it was a woman, man, or child. And they could not defend themselves. If they did, their case for asylum would get delayed.

Later that day, in the early evening, a lot of Kyegegwa District policemen from outside of the camp came into Kyaka II. Then things really got bad. When people saw the policemen, the protests escalated—there was more shouting, more violence. Things got out of control.

The policemen began beating people and throwing tear gas at them. The tear gas canisters exploding sounded like guns. This scared people and they ran from town to hide in houses and gardens. I remember lying down where we cooked, praying and asking God for forgiveness because I was convinced it was my last day on earth. Tibasima was in town with some of her friends to see the chaos for herself, and I was praying that God would protect her. I told my siblings, "We survived the war back home, but we are not going to survive this one."

I could hear people running outside our house, coming to the door, yelling "Open!" We did not open the door. It was just too scary. We were not well-liked in the refugee camp—people could tell by our features that we were of more than one tribe—and we feared some people would use the chaos as an opportunity to murder us. If that sounds like an overreaction, remember that only years before, we'd fled our homes because people killed other people they hated.

But it was Tibasima. She had to yell and say who she was before we opened the door. Her pants were all muddy. She ran inside, scared, but at the same time she was laughing—it turned out that she had fallen in a hole as she ran home. Sometimes, all you can do when things go wrong is laugh.

I lay on the ground next to the others with a hoodie covering my head and tears dripping off my face. We could hear tear gas canisters zipping through the air and then exploding and people yelling, screaming, and even knocking on our door, asking for water. Our roof was made of canvas and could burn down if a grenade-style tear gas canister landed on it. I prayed to God to protect us. It started getting cold on the floor, and I wanted to lift my head and change position. For a moment I could not feel my legs and my hands. I felt so ready for death.

When everything started calming down, Tibasima opened the door slowly. Standing in the middle of the doorway, she put her head outside and looked left and right, peering down both sides of the house. She stepped outside, went all around the house, and came back in.

"You can get up now," she said. "So you thought today was your last day?" she laughed.

"Yes," I said as my siblings started laughing with her.

I got mad. I wanted to walk away and go outside, but she told me I wasn't allowed to leave until tomorrow.

"If you are going to use the bathroom, you have to go with two or three people," she instructed us.

Later that night, my eldest brother Badulu came home. We were all so surprised since Badulu had to work and couldn't come home often.

"So you almost died today?" he said.

I do not even remember how I felt about him coming home because I was still emotionally recovering from the tear gas. I know I greeted him and told him to sit on the bench while I sat on the floor. We explained what was going on and asked if he had seen or heard from Alfred. He said he hadn't seen him in months and thought he was at home with us.

Badulu called the number he last used to speak to Alfred, but it didn't go through. Tibasima and Badulu were worried. I knew he would turn up somewhere; I had faith that he would be alive.

A few days later, the policemen set a curfew for the entire camp: After 7 p.m. no one should be outside. If they caught you outside, they would shoot or hit you.

"You're not going to go to school," Tibasima told us the next day. That morning, we did not go fetch water, we just did chores inside the house and none outside. Badulu tried to call Alfred again but couldn't reach him. He was so worried.

Curfew went on for a week. There was nothing much going on, not even the music that the club in town usually played every night and day. Policemen were everywhere, watching everyone. People felt uncomfortable in their own homes.

After trying and failing to reach Alfred, Badulu decided to go look for him. He left his phone with Tibasima, saying, "I will be calling you here so we can keep in touch."

After a week of policemen occupying the refugee camp, they left. Finally, people could breathe in their own homes. But the refugee office did not give people food for another month. We had to survive off what we grew in our gardens—corn, cassava, and a few vegetables—but as more and more refugees had come to Kyaka II over the years, the space for gardens was shrinking and not everyone could grow food. We counted on the refugee office for things like beans, flour, oil, more corn, sugar, and salt.

Many people were still recovering emotionally from being shelled with tear gas. The sound of tear gas canisters exploding—so much like gunfire—opened old wounds for some people. They said they couldn't sleep, plagued by nightmares of gunfire.

After two weeks, we finally heard from Badulu. He had found Alfred, but the rest of his news was not good. Alfred was in jail. Badulu worked hard to get Alfred out of jail and finally did, although he never really explained how he made that happen. I was scared and didn't sleep that night, a lot of what-ifs running through my mind, thinking how Alfred must be feeling and wondering if Badulu had not gone, what would have happened. A week later, they both returned home, and finally we all were together in one place. It was a joy to see them both home, but it was short-lived. After a month, they left the camp to go find work again.

I thought life at the refugee camp wouldn't ever get easier. Each day felt like I was getting closer to the day of death. Nothing seemed to go in our favor; it felt like the world was against us, that the world did not like me. There were days when I felt useless, hopeless, and not worthy of any love. But I knew I had to keep fighting for my family because I was not alone. Even if everything was not going our way, at the end of the day, we had each other. Somehow we always got through it together.

4

TIBASIMA'S WAR

ONE HOT AFTERNOON WHEN I WAS ABOUT TEN, my younger brother, Tusiime, and I were washing clothes at the stream. My older sister, Zawadi, came, I thought so that she could fetch water. As she walked down the hill, I saw on her face that she was scared.

When she reached us, she said, "There is a man at home who is trying to hurt Tibasima."

"Why?" I asked.

She said, "He is complaining about his daughter, but I don't know why."

Immediately, I was worried—this was not the first time a man had beat up Tibasima.

Five minutes later, my younger sister, Irini, came running down the hill. As she ran, she yelled, "Desange, a man is beating up Tibasima!"

This time I did not spend time asking why. I ran up the hill, and my siblings ran after me, the water Zawadi planned to fetch forgotten. Because we had been washing clothes, I was in a very short skirt and open blouse. Irini asked if I was going like that, but I did not respond. I just ran.

People stared as we ran to save Tibasima. Irini was crying. I started crying, too. I knew there was nothing I could do; I was just going to feel helpless again.

I got to our house and saw people standing in the doorway or trying to stop the man. My first thoughts were of how I could stop him—could I get a knife and stab him? Tibasima was in the living room crying and bleeding. In between blows, she told me to run to town and call "the boys," our friends from the same tribe as Tibasima who were like family. I ran crying and found two of them sitting in the restaurant. I told them to get up and run through the gardens to get to my house to save Tibasima. As they ran, they called other boys to help. They got there fast and wanted to fight the man, but other people there held them back. The boys warned the man beating up Tibasima to leave her alone, and he ran away.

One of the boys cried after seeing how badly Tibasima was beaten. Tibasima needed to get to the hospital, so one of the boys put her on a motorcycle and drove her out of the camp, neighbors and friends following behind. My siblings and I could not go with her, but we knew she was in good hands. There was nothing we could do but return to our chores, which had to be done. Irini stayed with Zawadi, who was fixing dinner. Tusiime and I went back to the stream to finish washing our clothes.

We had no adult to stay with us, and there was a real possibility the man or his friends and family could come back to the house. The boys told us not to sleep in the house that night, so we stayed at Tibasima's friend's house. Later, the boy who drove the motorcycle came to where we were staying and told us that Tibasima had him take her to the police station instead of the hospital because she wanted to report the assault. But the man who beat up Tibasima got to them first and bribed the police to put her in prison.

The boy told us more about Tibasima's injuries: One of her teeth was knocked out and her face was swollen. I did not think she was going to live. We all collapsed into tears as the fear of losing Tibasima overwhelmed us. That first night I could not fall asleep. I was sure I would be killed because violent retaliation was sadly all too common in the refugee camp.

The boys visited the next day to check on us and took clothes for Tibasima to change into and food for her to eat. At the jail, they cleaned her up as best they could. The boys tried everything they knew to do, but they could not convince the police to let her go to the hospital.

Later that night, she passed out. Another prisoner in the cell with her started yelling and crying, and the police rushed Tibasima to the hospital where the boys were waiting (although I don't know who told them Tibasima was being taken there). They kept the woman whom we stayed with updated on Tibasima's condition so that we knew what was going on. The doctor had Tibasima transferred to a larger hospital the next day because she was in such a bad state. Two boys went with her and the other two stayed to try to figure out how to help. The police wanted to put the two boys who weren't at the hospital in prison, but they ran and hid. The police told Tibasima's friend to not let us children go anywhere, even out of the house. Tensions in the refugee camp were always high, but this fight between the man and Tibasima made things much worse. People in the refugee camp chose sides. It was getting out of control.

I felt helpless. I cried day and night, and my eyes became red and swollen. My siblings and I fasted. While this was happening, my two oldest brothers, Babulu and Alfred, were away working, and no one knew how to get ahold of them. We only went outside to go to the bathroom—even then, we were covered from head to toe so we would not be recognized. I felt like I was in prison and I would never find peace. My siblings and I were hated everywhere we went. It felt so dark inside—I was mad and hopeless, trying to find someone to blame for everything.

After long, painfully scary days, we heard from the boys that Tibasima was doing better. That gave me hope that she would survive. Time went by and things started calming down. My siblings and I finally went back home to our house after two weeks in total hiding with Tibasima's friend. Two days later, Tibasima came back home, but her face was still recovering. Once she was home, I breathed; I was happy to see her back home, but I was still mad. And she was a changed person—she became very careful about who was around her. Plus, we were all worried about how an incident like this would affect our case for asylum—our only way to leave the refugee camp.

. . .

We returned to school the week after she came home. One day, a policeman showed up at school. My teacher pulled me out of class, and the police officer took me outside. We sat under a tree and talked. It was a hot day, so it felt nice to get out of the class of 150 people and sit under a tree where the air was less stifling—at the refugee camp, only a few primary schools served hundreds of children, and one teacher would have a class of about a hundred kids.

It may have been a relief to be in the open air, but I was scared. I thought it strange that the police would question me and not my older sister.

The policeman said, "You are not in trouble, but I want to ask you something about the fight that was at your house."

"What about it?" I said, and before he could respond, I asked, "Does Tibasima know you came here to talk to me?"

All he said was, "I am on your side, you know that."

He made me nervous, and it was starting to get hot under the tree. I told him I needed to go to the bathroom, just so I could get away for a moment. He said I could, but added, "Do not run away. You are in big trouble."

"Okay," I said and went to the bathroom. It was so hot and humid, the air felt sticky. I felt overwhelmed. But I knew I couldn't stay there long, so I got out and reluctantly went back to the policeman.

He asked, "Do you remember what happened on the day that Tibasima was hit by the man?"

I explained that I was not there.

"Who do you think was in the wrong?" he asked.

"I do not know," I said. Who was I to judge? But I knew he was trying to get me to say something that would make Tibasima look bad.

"Can I take you to court to tell the truth?" he asked.

I said I would go.

Our conversation continued for about thirty minutes. He offered me a lollipop at one point, but I said no. To that, he said, "You are not a normal kid."

"If you were in my shoes, I do not think you would be normal either," I replied.

"You are so engaged in the conversation and so interested in what I'm going to say next."

He kept asking questions over and over. I felt like he kept questioning me just to see what he could get me to say. I avoided answering most of the time but did answer some of his questions. I was so flustered, I was getting a little confused.

He asked, "Do you like going to school here?"

I said, "Yeah," even though I wanted to tell him that I did not learn anything at school. I came to waste time and watch out for my siblings because other kids picked on us. But it wasn't worth bringing up; he couldn't change anything.

"I hear that you are the meanest person."

"That is not new to me," I said, getting annoyed. He was asking about things that did not concern him. I was so ready to be done with the conversation. He just kept pushing buttons if he didn't get what he wanted. It felt like he didn't see me as a kid, but instead as just a tool to get what he wanted.

"Next month will you come with me and Tibasima to court?"

I said okay, but inside I was terrified. I almost peed on myself. He made me feel like if I went to court, I would go to jail and never come back to my siblings.

"Do not be scared. If you testify to what you told me, you'll be fine. But I do hope you are not hiding anything." Finally, he looked at me and said, "You're a really smart kid. I am sorry you have to go through this. Just know I'm on your side even when you do not believe me. I know everyone thinks you guys are the bad ones. Just know people are afraid of what you have within you. You are bright. You are a very interesting person. I hope you find yourself one day and you remember these words. Thank you for not being scared of me and talking to me."

I did not say thank you back because I was sure he was trying to use me. So many people have come to authority and power like him but have ended up using me. I deeply appreciated his nice words in my heart, but I could not show that. I did not understand why he said kind things to me. No one had ever called me smart or interesting. All that people saw in me was evil.

I stayed under the tree. I cried my heart out that day, releasing so many emotions. I cried into the wind and blew my tears out, leaving my face streaked with tear marks. I did not cry because he saw something good in me; I cried because I knew that next month when I had to testify in court, I'd go to prison with Tibasima. I would lose my siblings, and I'd never see them again. I had no doubts about that.

I stayed under the tree for about fifteen minutes, then I walked back to my class. My teacher started joking about the policeman wanting to talk to me because I must have killed someone. I joked back saying, "You better come bail me out."

Another teacher wanted to know what the policeman talked to me about, but I said that I did not want to discuss it. Yet another teacher asked if I had been crying.

"Why do you ask that?" I said.

"Your face is wet," he said.

"The mean girl never cries," I replied.

After school, I asked my siblings if a policeman had talked to them. They said no, and I told them what happened. I told them they could not tell anyone.

"Are you planning to tell Tibasima?" they asked.

"No, why would I?" I asked. "If I tell her, she'll beat me or ask more questions about it. I've already had enough questions for the day."

I told my siblings that I cried, surprising them. When I was beaten at school by teachers and at home by Tibasima, I would never cry.

Tusiime said, "If you cried, it must be serious."

"Do not focus on me crying, focus on the fact that you may not see me the rest of your life," I said to him. I think this scared all of them, but they tried not to show it.

My siblings and I walked home very slowly, practicing how we were going to face Tibasima and not tell her anything about the policeman.

When we got home, Tibasima asked me if the police questioned me at school. She said she knew that the police wanted to talk to me.

"Why didn't you come, then?" I asked. I couldn't believe she had let me face the policeman alone.

"He told me to stay here so you could 'see the truth,'" she said.

It had been such a long day, and I did not want to talk about it at all. But Tibasima kept asking what I told the policeman.

"I told him the story that you already know," I said.

"You know you're going to have to go to court and testify?" she asked.

"Yeah I know, the policeman told me," I replied.

"You know if you mess up, we're both going to jail."

"Yes, I know that," I said.

Tibasima told me I had to practice my testimony every day after school. We kept talking like that, and I tried to show her I wasn't worried about it. But deep down I was so scared. Every time I thought about it, I wanted to pee in my pants. I just wanted the conversation to stop, but Tibasima kept saying the same things. I said less and less.

Finally, she asked, "Is everything okay? Did the policeman do something to you?"

I said no, then blurted out the question that had been distressing me as much as the possibility of going to jail. "Why me and not anyone else?" I asked. "Why did the police choose me to testify on your behalf but not my siblings?"

"Don't ask me. Ask the policeman when you see him next time," she said, loud and frustrated, as if my question was missing the point. To her, maybe so, but it was important to me.

For a month, I anxiously waited for the day I might see the police-man again. The whole time, Tibasima constantly asked me, "Are you practicing your testimony?"

I said, "Yes, as always," every time.

I felt like my testimony was going to be everything to the court. But who would believe a kid unless money was offered? And the opposite could happen—someone could bribe the judge to send us to prison just like they bribed the police to put Tibasima in jail before.

I was carrying a responsibility—Tibasima's freedom—that I didn't want and that I should not have had to shoulder. I waited and waited for the policeman to come take Tibasima and me to court. For a whole month, I waited. But I never heard from or saw him again. And after the month passed, I was relieved, and could finally stop trying to memorize my testimony.

At the time, I didn't know why this fight started. It didn't make sense to ask because I knew I was never going to be told the truth because I was a child. Years later, the true story came out. Tibasima had a male friend in the camp who had come from Iraq. He liked a girl in the camp, and Tibasima allowed them to meet in secret in our home. The girl's brother came looking for her, but Tibasima lied and said the couple wasn't there. Then, the girl's father came and saw the girl's shoes by the door. The father tried to break in, but Tibasima held him back while signaling to the couple to escape. The father turned his rage on Tibasima, and while he beat her, the couple got away.

This incident made me think about many things. People in the camp chose sides of this fight only because of the tribe they affiliated with; they knew nothing about how the fight started. The people on Tibasima's side thought no man should ever hit a woman like that. The man who hit Tibasima had no mercy for Tibasima or his daughter for the choices they made. He acted like he was king—even when he left the house running, he still acted proud of what he'd done. Everyone was so quick to judge each other and throw away all the relationships that they had built over many years. It all reminded me of a passage in the Bible:

> *Do not judge, or you too will be judged. For in the same way you judge others, you will be judged, and with the measure you use, it will be measured to you. Why do you look at the speck of sawdust in your brother's eye and pay no attention to the plank in your own eye? How can you say to your brother, "Let me take the speck out of your eye," when all the time there is a plank in your own eye?* (Matthew 7, New International Version)

5

IT TAKES A VILLAGE

BY THIS TIME, LIFE WAS GETTING HARD. I wanted to escape my world in my mind, so I could not concentrate on school. I needed a change.

A few years earlier, when I was about eight or nine, a woman Tibasima knew from a nearby village had gotten permission from Tibasima to take me home with her to babysit her children, promising to also send me to school. This was a pretty common practice between family members or close family friends. I only lasted a few weeks before I got sick and had to go back to camp. I couldn't eat, I had diarrhea and vomiting, and everyone was worried. The doctors determined I'd developed ulcers from years of not having enough to eat and the stress of camp life. That our main food was corn flour didn't help since corn flour aggravates ulcers. I've had to be careful not to let them flare up ever since.

I tried babysitting again when I was about ten, but after a couple of months, I ran away from that family because they mistreated me, and I returned to camp. Even though babysitting hadn't worked twice, I knew it was a way to get away, and so I determined to try again.

I asked Tibasima if I could go back to a village and start babysitting. First, she told me she would think about it. After three weeks, I asked again, and she finally said yes. I took the bus, or walked, or got rides to different villages and would knock on doors to see if anyone needed a babysitter. If they said yes, I would stay. If they treated me poorly, I would leave and try the next village.

Soon I came to a village called Kayanja next to the lake that bordered both Uganda and Congo. The village was a long way from the camp, and it was unusual to me because it had mountains behind it but there were no trees. It was like the village was in an ocean of grass instead. People kept cows here, and people led their cows to the lake for their water. But they had to check the shallow area by the shore for crocodiles first and scare away any beasts that were there. Sometimes cows would go in the lake to drink water, and the crocodiles would try to catch them, and people would have to save their cow. If they could get the cow to land, it would be safe; the crocodile wouldn't try to fight the cow on land. Sometimes the lake would overflow, and the water would create other small lakes. Those times the entire village would become muddy, and houses could be flooded.

I met two beautiful women in Kayanja, and the village became my home. One was a grandma and the other was her daughter, who had four kids. I called them by the traditional respectful terms of endearment that fit their stations: I called the grandma Amooti and the daughter Abwooli.

Abwooli was a single mother raising four kids on her own. At sixteen, her parents took her out of school and had her get married. We both came from tribes where girls are not valued; they are merely products.

Abwooli said she really suffered in this marriage. Her husband never really provided anything, using the money they had on things that did nothing to help them. He never thought of a future; he just thought of the moment. And finally, one day, Abwooli's husband just walked away, so she and her children returned to her parents. Occasionally her husband would come to her parents' house, but just to see the kids and give them token little presents.

She told her story with her whole heart, and listening to it made me cry. I could tell she was trying to heal and let go. I loved that Abwooli was a hardworking woman who did not like nonsense. She was very bold and went for things she wanted; she did not sit around and wait for anything.

Amooti did not talk too much but was a good listener. She was a very smart woman but did not like conflict. She put everything on the line for her grandchildren. She sold all her cows, one by one, to make sure her grandchildren had something to eat, could afford to go to school, and could have a good Christmas.

We did our morning prayers together as a family. I loved that Amooti and Abwooli showed their children to start their day by praying to God, creating a greater foundation for their kids.

· · ·

One day, I was talking to Abwooli's oldest daughter, Kasiime, as we walked to collect firewood, and she told me the story about why she was raised by Amooti when she was little instead of Abwooli.

"When I was little, I used to faint a lot," she said. "Grandma Amooti came to visit me when I was sick and worried I would not make it. She talked to my grandpa who then told my dad that I should live with Grandma Amooti so she could take care of me. But my dad's father intervened and said no, that I would get better."

Kasiime explained that Amooti did not push it. In this culture you cannot talk back to men; whatever they say goes. Amooti left, and after a couple days, Kasiime fainted again, and the family relented. After a week of Amooti caring for her, Kasiime was better and never fainted again.

"Sometimes I think my grandmother has magic," she said. "And I am blessed to have Abwooli as my mother. She is a woman who has been through so much, yet she still stays positive. She believes in me and sent me to school, believing education is the key to life."

I could see how grateful she was for these women. She told me more about what they had been through.

"Mother Abwooli's father did not like Mom and never respected her or Grandma Amooti. He never really accepted us and always accused my siblings of stealing his things, which hurt Mother Abwooli," she said. "It broke my heart to see how he treated Grandma Amooti and Mother Abwooli and how hard they both worked to make sure my siblings and I have a better future. It's heartbreaking when Grandma Amooti gets sick and she has to sell her cows to pay for hospital bills," Kasiime said, tears streaming down her face.

Amooti had seven kids, but none of them really cared about her. Amooti and Kasiime's grandfather were estranged, and only Abwooli was willing to take care of her. Abwooli's sisters were married, and husbands rarely gave money to help a wife's family. Amooti's sons were rich and could have afforded to take her to the hospital when she was sick and needed medicine, but they didn't. It made me think they were heartless or that something was wrong with them.

Her eyes were so red from crying, and I could really see how she was hurting. I felt for her, I cried with her, and I told her, "That is out of your control. The only way to help these two women is to get educated and push yourself. The pain you have in your heart, use that, let it be a motivation. Don't let it send you backwards."

That day we ended up not collecting firewood. Instead, we shared our problems. We talked about the future. I shared with her that if I did get an education, I would use every opportunity to create opportunities for others to get an education, too. I told her how grateful I was for Abwooli and Amooti and how I'd never had two people believe in me like they do.

"They never just believe in anyone, they believe in those who have potential," she said.

"If God does bless me with money, they are the people I am looking for first," I said, already wanting to repay Abwooli and Amooti for their kindness.

We talked about marriage. I told her I hated how girls are sold like cows, that we were viewed as an income and do not get a say in whom we get married to, and that the whole village believed my only purpose was to get married. It hurt me so much to think I would not get to do anything with my life.

"I hate these men who think they are in control of the world," I told her. "I would rather fight and change the world with the people that believe in my vision than marry a man that would never see any value in me."

"Mother Abwooli and Grandma Amooti believe in education. They will not want to send me off to a marriage. They would fight for me like a lion fights for food. They have given me a safe world, and I do not have to worry about marriage like you," Kasiime said.

What she said really hit me. I wished I had someone who would fight for me like that. Tibasima might fight for me some, but I did not think she loved me enough to put her life on the line for me.

We sat in the hot sun and I cried, Kasiime watching me. Then she said, "You and I may not be blood, but we are family."

I told her about being called meaningless and worthless. She broke into tears and said, "I hope you find hope and strength in yourself and get to become the beautiful woman who is in you, because that woman is what the world is waiting for. People like you are the people that bless lives. You come from nothing, but God will make you into something."

· · ·

In some households in Africa, crying is seen as a weakness. Growing up, we were taught to not cry but to woman up—to stand stronger and keep our heads up no matter what. You were only allowed to cry when someone died.

For years, I rarely cried. Even when I was beaten by Tibasima, I would not cry. Later on, I came to understand that I had held so much inside.

That night after talking to Kasiime, I could not fall asleep. My thoughts were everywhere. I cried in the middle of the night. I felt so lonely. I had lost hope. I went to the kitchen—a small structure apart from the main house—and I knelt down in the dark, cramped room and prayed out loud.

"Oh, Heavenly Father, today I come with a heavy heart. I am so broken in pieces. Why did you have to let my life be this hard? Why me, Lord? Do you even really love me?"

I started yelling louder.

"Take me if I have no use, Lord. The world seems to think so, but you keep me here. For what, Lord, so I can be laughed at or so I can feel all this pain? Lord, show me a sign that you love me. Show me a sign this suffering will end. Lord, help me."

I did not know Abwooli and Kasiime could hear me in the main house. They both came out to me and said, "You know He loves you because you are alive. You still have a purpose. That is why you are still here. Your suffering will be your testimony one day."

Kasiime said, "There will be a point in life where people will try to put you down, but they will not be able to. You will stand strong like Mount Zion."

"Thank you for accepting me and letting me be a part of your life," I told them. "I don't want to sleep." I was wet with tears, my T-shirt drenched. They went to bed, and I stayed in the kitchen for the whole night.

I just told myself it would be okay. That night I looked around in the dark and said all the things that I was grateful for, and that changed my mood. I remember going outside at 6 a.m. and watching the sunrise. It was a beautiful end to a night of crying and praying.

That night I came to understand it is okay to be hated or talked bad about, as long as you do not let it affect you. The only opinion that matters in the end is mine alone. Since that night, I have wanted to never let anyone walk all over me. It didn't matter if it was family or close friends. I needed to say enough is enough.

· · ·

Looking back, these are the two women who have made the most impact on me. They are my role models. They are so strong, and they stood against all the odds to raise four kids on their own.

In Amooti and Abwooli's family, I saw the men shirk responsibility.

Watching this situation made me mad, but there was nothing I could do. It really made me see the world differently after watching these two women raise four children on their own. They became father and mother. They became everything to the kids.

These women gave me a home that no one else could give me. I became their child. They gave me hope and fought for me like I was their own. I once asked them, "Why do you always see the good in me even when the world does not?"

They replied, "A mother will always see good in her child and believe in them no matter what. It is a mother's job to keep raising her child. We may not be related by blood, but you are our daughter. One day, you'll become this big person, and no one will believe it.

"The one thing you need to know is who you are! People will always have a different vision of you; you need to believe in yourself before anyone else can. You need to stay strong and trust God and know everything will work out.

"My child, " Amooti said, " you are the chosen one. Your path will come with a lot; you need to know bad times will come your way and you will be hated even by your own family. You need to stand and know you are not alone."

Amooti's words meant everything to me. She spoke to me like she had a vision of my life and knew exactly what was going to happen. In their hands, I felt loved like never before. These women believed in me and pushed me to become the best I could be. These two women became my earthly heroes.

I have come to understand something I've always been told: Family isn't always blood. It's the people in your life who want you in theirs. The ones who accept you for who you are. The ones who would do anything to see you smile, and who love you no matter what.

Looking back, I realize it definitely took a village to raise the person I am today. I reflect on all the women who took steps to be a mother figure in my life. As women, we never do it alone; we are a team and make things happen.

At this village, I learned about myself and how it feels to be loved. I learned what kind of woman I wanted to be. I left as a new person. But it would take a long time for that new person to be able to realize her dreams.

6

HOUSE ON FIRE

ONE HOT NIGHT IN THE BEGINNING OF 2012, we were sound asleep when we woke up to Tibasima screaming, "Wake up! Run outside!"

Our house was on fire. I started crying and then ran to our neighbors to get help. Tibasima tried to get things out of the house, but people held her back so she wouldn't go back into the flames. Others tried to douse the flames with water and soil.

Tears ran down my cheeks as I watched the house burn down. I did not have a home anymore. And the person who burned the house could be standing right there among the people who were trying to help. Many of our neighbors had not forgiven Tibasima for helping the two lovers connect. That she nearly lost her life when the girl's father beat her wasn't enough. They thought she was a bad influence on the young people in the camp, and they never liked us children for being from a mixed marriage. They wanted us gone. I cried without stopping, wondering, What next? Problems after problems, I felt like the queen of problems.

I sat outside all night watching the house burn—watching until everything turned to ash. I watched Tibasima worry and people feel sorry for us and give us clothes. People offered us food, but we threw it away, fearing it could be poisoned.

The refugee camp that was supposed to feel like home turned out to be a pit filled with lions ready to attack as soon as you turned your back. Everywhere you turned you saw a lion. After you finished killing one lion, another came out of nowhere without warning. We couldn't trust anyone, which is why Tibasima wouldn't ever tell others about the status of our case for asylum, for fear someone would go to bad witches and have them curse our case or go to the office and lie about us, making the office stop our case and investigate us.

Our lives were in danger. Danger that was out of our control. Danger that could kill one of us.

With no shelter, we slept outside by the gardens and in green banana trees. The nights were long and cold. Sometimes the wind drove sand into our eyes. I did not want to do anything for a week after our house burned down. I didn't want to talk to anyone. I was tired of going through these problems. There were days that I did not see the point of living anymore. I was truly giving up on life.

I could pretend on the outside it didn't bother me anymore. As far as anyone could tell, I didn't care. People saw that, and it made them even more bold, telling us they hated us to our faces. I told my siblings to ignore them because it wasn't worth it. My siblings and I needed to realize that the problem was not us, the problem was them. Everyone was grieving the family and friends they had lost and what they'd been forced to leave behind, and they were trying to blame their pain on someone.

Days went by, and one day, Tibasima went to Kampala, the capital of Uganda, and stayed there for a week. She didn't explain what she was going to do there, and I thought she'd left us forever, tired of all the problems we brought upon her.

When she got back, she told us she went to the office for the UN High Commissioner of Refugees. "They will be taking us out of this camp," she said. "Tonight."

We left the Kyaka II like thieves in the night. We did not say good-bye to anyone. Tibasima told us not to say anything, worried there were people who would fight us if they knew we were leaving the camp.

Zawadi and I sat by the road close to our garden full of corn, just looking at each other in the dark without saying anything. At that moment, I just wanted to know how she felt about moving. But we did not really know how to share our feelings or how we felt about things. Our silence answered the questions in each other's minds.

A big white van with blue stripes that would take us to Kampala neared the place that used to be our home. I was both excited and scared, knowing that even in Kampala we would face more problems and trouble, but I also did not want to stay in the refugee camp, because my life was on the line. Living in the refugee camp was hard, and my family and I left our mark there. I'm not sure if it was a good mark. I had to trust Tibasima; she had been there for us. I had to trust that this was another path we were on together and that we would survive it.

We all got into the big van, and Tibasima told us to sit in the back. She yelled at me because I said I wanted to sit in the front. I never really understood Tibasima. She never let us do anything we wanted. We were all quiet in the car. The driver tried talking to us, but no one wanted to talk. The driver gave up and drove back to the main road to pick up other people who were traveling to do business outside of the camp. Tibasima looked back and said, "Keep quiet and do not talk." It felt like we were hiding from someone.

I sat by the window with Zawadi next to me. Since we had to stay quiet, Zawadi and I used signs to communicate. We drove past the gardens filled with corn, and I stared out the window, looking at the moon. That night it was full and bright. I turned my body to the window and cried. I was so scared of this new change. Zawadi put her arm on my back, reminding me I was not alone.

On our journey to Kampala, we stopped in Mubende for food. People brought food to our window, and after I paid, I passed the food to my siblings. There was a lady in a blue dress and a red head wrap who held a white bucket on her head. When I put my hand outside of the van for my food, she held it and told me everything would be okay. It was like she felt my fear and all the emotions I was feeling that day. That moment stayed with me all day.

After seven long hours, we arrived at the hotel where we were going to stay until the office of refugees in Kampala found a home for us and took everything to our room. We had fun exploring everything until Tibasima yelled at us and said that these new things were just weird. It was just like her to dampen any hint of a good mood. Around Tibasima I could never really laugh. I always wanted to just get out of her sight.

Our hotel was close to a mosque, and we would hear them pray now and then. That day I was stress free. I did not have to worry about chores. It was a nice and warm evening, so I went outside of the hotel room. Then Tibasima started yelling at me. It seemed she always yelled at me, more than any of my other siblings. It made me feel like Tibasima never loved me, that she blamed me for anything that went wrong.

She told me she did not want me outside. Staying in that room, not being allowed to step out the door, felt like I was in prison. It was a feeling that would come to represent the rest of my time in Kampala.

7

LIFE IN LIMBO IN KAMPALA

AFTER TWO WEEKS OF LIVING IN THE HOTEL, we finally got a house. Kampala is a beautiful city, but it is so crowded. Our house was in a gated community in a ghetto very close to town. The house was nice. The floor was made of cement, and it surprised me how cold it felt on my bare feet the first time I walked inside the house with no shoes. Since there was no electricity, we used candles for light.

Everywhere outside the house was brown; we did not have any grass. The day we moved in, it rained, and the ground was so muddy. There was a big tree just outside the house, and the rain had knocked lots of leaves to the ground. Tibasima told us to sweep the leaves away. But it was muddy—how could I sweep leaves from mud? I stood at the doorway, staring at everything, feeling confused about so much more than just leaves and mud.

"Stop standing there and get to work!" Tibasima yelled.

She never talked to me calmly; she always yelled at me or hit me. That day I felt so sad. Things looked so bleak, I just wanted to go back to the refugee camp. Even though I knew the camp was dangerous for us, this didn't feel like an improvement.

Our house had one bedroom, a living room, and a place to cook. Tibasima and Irini slept in the bedroom, Tusiime slept in the living room, and Zawadi and I slept where we cooked. We'd clean the area after cooking, then put clothing down on top of the cement floor to sleep on, not just to make it softer, but because the heat from all the cooking made the floor feel hot. One night, Zawadi rolled over in her sleep and burned her nose on the small charcoal stove that hadn't yet cooled. Luckily it was not a bad burn, and we could laugh about it.

Our bathroom was outside, and the toilet did not have a door. To keep from surprising someone with their pants down, you had to yell to make sure it wasn't occupied before you got too close. It wasn't too nice to begin with, but when it rained, it got nastier in there. But we did have a shower in the house, which was a good thing.

We gathered fresh water from a nearby well. In the back of our house, there was a big hole where we could pour dirty water after doing dishes and laundry. Our backyard bordered a secondary school, and students would throw food leftover from their lunches into our backyard—it was gross. Worse, sometimes after they peed in water bottles (you know—teenagers!), they would toss the pee-filled bottles into our backyard, too.

There was an automobile repair shop in the complex with auto body parts scattered all around. I got to know the guys who fixed the cars when I would go out that way to fetch water or when Tibasima would send me and Zawadi to the little nearby store to get things like milk, salt, or corn. Sometimes those guys gave me money I'd use to buy food.

Badulu and Alfred were never really around. We only saw them two or three times a year. But they always called Tibasima to check in on how we were doing.

Tibasima still followed our case for asylum. It was something she made time for, even though big city life in Kampala was harder for her than life in the refugee camp. The refugee office only provided food to us for the first couple of months, just long enough in their minds for Tibasima and my older brothers to find jobs, but it was hard for them to find work. Despite the hardships, every week Tibasima went to the refugee office to check the status of our chance to leave Uganda for America, keeping the pressure on. Even though it seemed the refugee office was doing everything in its power to make sure we left Uganda, Tibasima wanted to show the office she would not give up.

After a month in the new house, my siblings and I started going to Nabagereka Primary School. Everyone was supposed to wear blue uniforms, but they cost money we didn't have, so my siblings and I went to school for about a year without them. Zawadi and I were sent home one day for not having a uniform, and of course, had to go back the next day still in our everyday clothes.

We got called into the school office and had to explain our situation. The teacher felt sorry for us, and I hated that. I do not like people's pity. I understand you feel for me, but do not look at me with eyes that show me you are thinking "poor kid." The next day our teachers got us uniforms, one set each. We washed our uniforms every day, but we did not mind, we were just grateful to have them. It was nice to finally be dressed like everyone else and not be embarrassed at school assemblies.

After a year of going to school, we stopped because we could not afford to pay the tuition. We started going to Bethel Healing Centre Church every weekday—the church was so close to where we lived we could hear people singing from our house. We would wake up each morning, do our chores, then spend the day at church singing, worshiping, praying, or simply watching people come and go. My favorite part of each day was praying and listening to people's testimonies. At the end of the day, about 6 p.m., we would go home, and Zawadi and I would then cook dinner for the family.

I found peace at Bethel Healing Centre Church. I really loved the spirit of the people there, although some people felt sorry for us, and I did not like the looks of pity they gave me and my siblings. Sometimes when I went to church, I never wanted to go back home. Tibasima always did something at home to make me uncomfortable—I do not know if she ever really knew this. Church felt more like home.

The church provided opportunities to meet people—especially kids my age—and get involved. I joined the church choir and often helped with the younger children in the choir. That pleased the choir leaders but caused some jealousy with the other teen girls. After choir practice one day, a girl and I got into a disagreement about something that happened in practice. She said, "You're so meaningless. Why do you try to fight about things that have no point?"

That word again. I tried to laugh it off and show it didn't hurt me for her to say that. "There's no point in me using my words with you, but I can show you the point of me with action." And I balled up my fists in a half-joking way. My siblings were there and encouraged me to leave. They knew if the girl kept provoking me, then the joke would be over fast.

But such incidents were rare at Bethel Healing Centre Church. Most people there were simply kind. One woman who worked in the church and sometimes led prayer during the week, Abeni, cooked food for me and my siblings. But when she called Zawadi and told her to tell us to come and eat, Zawadi said we were fasting—she didn't like pity, either.

Abeni was a very sweet lady, and she and I became close—so close that some people at church thought she was my mother. Sometimes we would sit on the top of the church, facing the nearby mosque, and talk as the sun set. She was a great listener. At times I could tell she was feeling sorry for me, but I always tried my best not to show her that I saw that. She never talked much about herself. Sometimes I got the feeling that someone hurt her deeply and she struggled to forgive them. Instead, she talked about how she viewed the world. Abeni always advised me to stay away from boys. She said she saw something big in me. I thought Abeni was a very interesting woman. You had to pay close attention to what she was telling you to really understand her.

Then, suddenly, she disappeared without saying goodbye. This hurt me deeply. I went to church a whole week without seeing her. I asked around and heard she returned to her village. I was very sad for a while. It felt like breaking up with someone.

On the days I stayed late at church talking, I would run home so I could beat Tibasima to our house. Sometimes I did not want to go to church, but Tibasima would force me. Tibasima is not someone who hears the word "no" or puts up with being talked back to—whatever she says goes. But that was hard for me to take. I almost always talked back.

Tibasima wanted me to be like Zawadi; she was always comparing us. Tibasima would say, "Zawadi is so sweet and quiet, she follows rules, she is patient, she is beautiful inside and out." To her, I was the rule breaker, the crazy one. If Tibasima blamed me unjustly, I stood up for myself, and I loved that about myself. But she made me feel like I was the worst kid on earth. Anything that I did was ugly to her. *I* was ugly to her. It felt like she found happiness in my tears and suffering.

Life in Kampala was getting harder and harder. I didn't like where we were living even though the house was better than the one we had in the refugee camp. We could escape to nature in the refugee camp; we could go outside and play, and Tibasima never worried where we were. In the big city, we were never allowed to play with other kids. Zawadi and I couldn't go play at all. Tibasima wanted Zawadi and me in the house, working. Kampala ended my childhood—I wish I'd had the freedom to be a child longer.

We did have rare moments when we got out of the house for reasons other than to spend the day at church. Sometimes I could go to villages to visit family members and friends. Sometimes Tibasima would tell me and Zawadi to get dressed and go with her to town. It was fun to not be in the house all day. Zawadi and I sometimes wore matching clothes. We were the same height, and people thought we were twins. But otherwise, life in Kampala felt to me like a prison.

My job was to do house chores and stay inside. If I went outside to play with other kids, I would be beaten until my body was swollen. In Africa, beating means you are being disciplined to learn manners and right from wrong. But these beatings were beyond what most adults do for discipline. Tusiime and Irini used to go outside and play when they got home from church or school. If she caught them, Tibasima would beat Tusiime but not Irini. I always wondered why Tibasima spared her. My only guess was that she felt most connected to Irini because she had raised her since she was an infant.

Zawadi and I cooked for the whole house every single day. Sometimes it felt like we were slaves. I did not have peace; my heart was always worried. I worked so hard to please Tibasima, hoping maybe she would like me and treat me a little better. She never appreciated anything I did. She told me the food I cooked was not good, that I did a bad job cleaning. She never recognized the effort I put in. I tried so hard for her to see me and hear my heart. But her words were like a sharp knife to my heart, and she knew it, so she used them to slice and stab as much as possible. And emotions would tumble down inside me like a crashing waterfall.

There were moments that I thought of running away. Sometimes things would go wrong at home, and Tibasima would immediately think it was my fault, even when it was not. Although I'm built to defend myself, sometimes I didn't, because what would be the point? If she already believed it was me, no one could change her mind. Out of all my siblings, I was the one who was beaten the most.

It got to the point where I would get beaten, and I would not even cry; I became numb to it. There were times when it felt like I was made of rocks—if you touched me, all you could feel were bumps.

Zawadi and I were very close. She was always there, offering a shoulder to cry on. I cried most nights. Crying helped me release the pressure and take a breath. Zawadi was like my therapist: She listened to me complain, sometimes telling me things would get better, sometimes just listening. We never really talked about how we felt about everything. We all knew that we were not okay with how we were treated, but for the sake of our future—our chance to leave Uganda and go to America—we had to stick it out. If it was not for Zawadi, I would have run away.

After we'd been in Kampala for about six months, the office of refugees brought two teenaged boys to stay with us. Personally, I did not like it. I just did not like the boys' vibes. I once got into a fight with one of the boys. He punched me in my eye, and it became extremely swollen. Tibasima took his side and told the boy he did a good job beating me up. She said this in front of other people. I couldn't help but think this sent the message that it was okay for anyone to beat us up. To her, we were meaningless. I knew then for sure what I guessed at the times I was assaulted at camp—I could never go to her for help. I knew she would never protect me.

After a while, the boys left the house. A couple months later, the refugee office no longer provided us with money for rent, and we were kicked out of the house. We started sleeping outside in empty shipping containers that people had outside of their shops. We'd spend the day at church or out and about, then sneak in at night, hoping no one saw us, and slept on the cold metal with just a blanket and nothing else. Then in the morning, we'd sneak out early, wash up at the well, and the days continued like that for about two weeks. What saved us was a kind man named Kahi David Amusavi.

. . .

Kahi David Amusavi was a lawyer at the refugee office. He was the one person that tried to look out for us children while we lived in Kampala. He was very kind, and he checked on us often. He was from Kenya, but he had a nice, big house in a nice neighborhood in Kampala. Worried for us, knowing we had no place to go, he invited us to move into his home.

I learned so much from Kahi. He made me feel I was loved. I used to write notes for him to show how much I appreciated him. Around his house there were flowers growing; I would sometimes cut the flowers and give them to him. He made me feel I had a purpose. Kahi felt like a father to me, and he was the best father I could ever ask for.

Most days, Kahi went to work in the morning, and when he came home, he taught us from the Bible. He never went to church, even though we always asked him to join us, but he knew the Bible well.

Once his wife from Kenya made a surprise visit. She didn't realize we were living with him, and when she found out, she didn't like it and was angry but tried not to show it. In African culture, you try to fake being okay so others do not notice your angry feelings. But Kahi made us a part of his family, despite her feelings. He treated us the way he would treat his own kids and even introduced us to much of his family.

While living with Kahi, Miracle Centre Cathedral became our new church. Irini and Tusiime joined the Proclaim Children's Choir Ministry, and I really loved the Sunday school. The pastor that was the Sunday school teacher welcomed me and my siblings with an open heart. He always made sure we had food. Sometimes we declined what he offered, but we appreciated his kindness. Another Sunday school teacher became a mentor to me; he encouraged me to preach during our Sunday school service and even taught me how to dance.

Barbara was one of the people I will never forget at that church. She was a friend and stood by us and protected us like she did her own sisters. When others talked badly about us behind our backs, she always defended us.

But even though I connected with these amazing people, I never felt like I belonged to that congregation. Everyone there spoke English, which we did not. And the church was very organized and structured. I missed the passion at Bethel Healing Centre, how they praised God with their whole heart. It was where I most felt at peace.

When we moved far away from Bethel Healing Centre, I always wanted to walk back to it each Sunday. But Tibasima wouldn't let me, because she suspected I had a boyfriend at church, which wasn't true.

In both churches, I met amazing people—people who accepted me and my siblings and truly helped us. But there were also people who promised us things—like helping us with our education—and did not deliver. I wished they had never promised anything. Instead, I wish they had just tried to be our friends. That would have meant a lot to us.

While we lived with Kahi, Tibasima did not beat us up. I do not know why, but it seemed she was scared of him. Despite this, she still used harsh words with us, but Kahi didn't know, because he didn't speak our language of Kihema. We mostly communicated with him through Swahili, which we all spoke. But when he was away, Tibasima could treat us like she did before. Once, when he was away on a trip to Kenya, I stole a few coins, less than a few dollars' worth, and bought little things like ice cream. It was just a rebellious moment. Tibasima caught me and beat me for a long time, all the while telling me how much I embarrassed her.

Then Kahi lost his job, and it was very stressful for him. He really worried about us as well as for himself. What were we going to eat? I really hated seeing him worried. But we always told him, "Do not worry, the Bible tells us not to worry about what you will eat tomorrow." (Matthew 6:25–27)

After Kahi got a new job, we could afford food again, but our time living together had to end. Kahi could no longer afford the large house and moved to a smaller home. Tibasima found an apartment for us that she could afford that was also near Kahi's new home. Luckily, our new home was nearby, and so we could visit him any time. But soon, Kahi returned to Kenya, and we moved to the other side of the city into a one-bedroom apartment Tibasima found for the five of us to live in. We attended a nearby church, and that congregation helped us go to school once more.

After we came to America, we stayed in touch with Kahi. Unfortunately, he passed away two years after we settled in the US. He was sick for only a week when he passed away. When they told me he was gone, it was like a bomb dropped on me. I couldn't believe it. I could not sleep that night. I went to bed and all I could think about was his face and the wonderful time we spent with him. I wish I was given one more chance to visit him and talk about our past and laugh about it.

All I could do was ask myself, "Why don't good people last in this world?" I went on Facebook and read all the comments people were posting about him, and all I could do was cry. He was not only good to us, but to a lot of people. He touched many lives. It is hard to find a heart like his in this world.

I'll never forget his kindness. Kahi saw us for who we were in a time when most people saw us as nasty. From Kahi, we learned how to help other people and to never give up, no matter what comes your way. To him, it didn't matter your tribe or where you came from—if someone needs help and you can help, step up and do what you can and use what money you have in a way that makes a difference.

Kahi David Amusavi, you're going to be missed and you're going to be loved forever in our hearts. Hold on tight—we will meet again.

8

OUR AMERICAN JOURNEY

OUR HOPE THE ENTIRE TIME WE WERE REFUGEES in Uganda was to come to America and find a good life. On October 15, 2014, when I was thirteen, our dream came true.

That day, I was coming home from school, and I was so tired. Irini ran up to me in the street, barefoot and giggling and so happy. She punched me hard on my arm.

"What was that for?" I asked.

"We are going to America!" she yelled as she ran away, taking my backpack with her so I'd have to follow her. When I caught up to her, I punched her back and said, "Next time try to control your excitement."

She'd run to a nearby shop to get a treat to celebrate, but I didn't go in. I did not believe what my little sister told me. I didn't want to get my hopes up only to be disappointed later. Why now after all these years? Each new year, we always said, "This is our year to go to America." Tibasima would do a lot of shopping, and we would all get ready to go like we were leaving the next day. But the year would end, and we would not be in America.

I walked home, and when I got there, Tibasima told me that our visas came and that we would leave for America in two weeks. I knelt down and cried for five minutes while praying and thanking God for the visa.

That night, we all had different emotions. Zawadi was quiet. "Do you really believe it?" she asked me.

"My hopes are not up," I responded. "That's the best I can give you right now. I am still processing it."

Tusiime was excited but tried to act like he did not care. Irini was very happy. Tibasima was so happy she got dressed up and went out to celebrate with friends, which I found rude.

I just kept believing, hoping, and praying.

. . .

A few days before our flight to the US, we left our apartment at around 10 p.m. to go to a hotel near the airport. Once again, Tibasima spirited us away under the cover of night.

Two motorcycles carried us and our few things to the hotel. Tibasima was on one, and us four kids were on another—Irini on the front between the driver and the handlebars and the rest of us behind the driver. The moon was full and bright, and I looked around the neighborhood as we left. I felt sad, with so many other emotions, too. This journey felt like it was another dream that we were going to wake up from.

The next morning, Tibasima actually let us sleep in! We started taking malaria medication to be ready to come to America. After we ate, Tibasima left the hotel for a while and left us there, and we just played. The days we spent in the hotel were days that I truly felt hope and had faith in the process. But I tried to temper my expectations. I would go outside, sit in the sun, and worry they were lying to us. So many times we had talked about and prepared for going to America, only to have nothing come of it. But what crossed my mind was that I really was leaving everything behind—a home that I had known for thirteen years.

I started imagining how life would be in America, how my deep desire for an education would come true. Most people in my culture believed there was no value in girls attending school, that girls should focus instead on tending the house and preparing for marriage. But I always knew they were wrong. I longed to get educated. I knew that if I could read and write, my place in life would be meaningful.

Doubt took over my thoughts. I was leaving Africa. Since I was a young child, I had been looking for a home to belong to. I did not know if this new country would really accept me. As a refugee, I did not know if I would ever find a country that would really accept me. What is the point of even trying to go to America? I may end up not doing anything with my life. I just had to keep telling myself: Education is my key. Trust God and let Him do His magic. He got you to this point. Know that He will get you though.

The day we left, people called to say goodbye, but I did not really want to say goodbye over the phone because most people were crying when they called, and I was trying not to cry. When we got to the airport, we got off the bus, collected our bags, and loaded them onto a cart. We waited outside for almost an hour saying goodbye to people whom Tibasima had invited to come see us off. The office of the International Organization for Migration (IOM) came and started calling names for each family and giving papers and bags needed for travel. Once we were inside the airport and past security, we looked back through the airport's glass wall and saw our friends and family—some who had arrived too late to say goodbye—crying as they watched us go. All we could do was wave at them. It made me feel so sad, but I did not cry.

. . .

We arrived in Utah in the afternoon on October 17, 2014. We got lost in the airport at first—which seems funny now because the airport was so small then—but there was a white man who directed us where to go. This was a big moment. Not only had we stepped foot into our new country, we were meeting our new family.

Badulu was an adult, and so it fell to him and Tibasima to work out our plans for America with the Office for Refugees and Immigrants. Alfred was old enough to make his own choices, but the rest of us minor children were going into foster care managed by a faith-based agency. The refugee office said it would be easier for us to finalize coming to America if we were split up to live with different families. Not only would that speed up the process because it would be easier for the agency to find foster families that could take one or two children instead of four together, but it would allow Tibasima and Badulu to settle in if they did not have to be responsible for us. But luckily, kindly, our new foster family agreed to take us all together.

And so at the airport, we had to say goodbye to Tibasima, Badulu, and Alfred. We were going different ways and starting this new life away from each other. Tibasima told me to be a good kid, listen, learn good behavior, and leave the bad behavior behind. We had a translator with us who told us that we would see each other again at some point. That gave me hope.

There to meet us at the airport was our new foster family—Arnie and Ilene Smith and two of their seven kids, Abigail and Billy. We also met our caseworker, Emma, who became more of a mother figure to us, and the manager of the foster care program at that time.

I was excited, sad, and scared. I was excited to stop getting yelled at all the time and being blamed for the things that I did not do. I was excited for peace. But at the same time this was a new world. I was not sure if the family we were going to leave with was going to really protect us.

9

MY NEW WORLD

WE DROVE TO THE SMITHS' HOME, which was in a suburb of a bigger city. I did not cry, but I was scared. I did not know where Tibasima and my brothers were going to live, and I did not even have a phone to call them. As we drove home on the freeway, the cars were fast. I was fascinated by the roads, which seemed to be doing a tango with each other.

Arnie and Ilene told us we could call them by their first names, but we called our foster parents Mom and Dad immediately because Tibasima told us that was the way for us to show them respect. In our culture, it's inappropriate to call your elders by their first name.

Arnie dropped us off at home and went back to work. Ilene, the kids, Emma the caseworker, and a translator gave us a tour of our new home. The first thing they showed us was our room. Tusiime was going to share a bedroom with Billy, our new brother. We girls were going to share a room that had three beds, and we all chose which bed we would sleep in. I chose the bed that was close to the window because it had a rainbow-colored blanket that I liked. Our closet was full of clothes and shoes. The two Smith daughters that lived at home had their own room. The other four Smith children were grown and out of the house.

We put our bags in the closet, then we went to the bathroom, and they started explaining how everything worked. That made me mad—we'd already figured out bathrooms—but I stayed quiet to not make a big deal. When they began to explain feminine pads, I really got mad and ashamed because our translator was a man. From there we moved on to the kitchen where we tried some food. I did not like most of it. I especially did not like pizza—I knew nothing about cheese, and that melted stretchy stuff was just too weird. It took me three months before I was willing to try it. They showed us the rest of the house and the garage—I'd never seen big doors that open themselves before.

Eventually our caseworker and translator left. We decided to play outside. It was sunny out, and so we automatically changed into shorts, because at home, sunny always meant warm. But this was October in Utah. It felt so cold! It didn't feel cold to our foster family, but for me and my siblings, it was freezing. We stayed in our shorts but grabbed our coats. When Arnie came home from work, I ran to him and gave him a hug and said, "Welcome back home, Dad!"

Over the next few days, we got to know our foster family. Arnie and Ilene were kind, almost always treated us like their own children, and grew to love us. Arnie was a very interesting man. He was very calm, a good listener, and good at putting himself in other people's shoes to try to understand them. He did not talk much, but he loved to joke around. Arnie was also very protective when it came to his family.

One foster sister was Sarah. She would always dance with us in the kitchen. She was so kind and outgoing, and she did nice things for us. It felt like she completely understood us and tried to put herself in our shoes, but later she would become upset that our actions hurt her mom.

Our foster brother Billy was someone I didn't really get along with; we always butted heads. Whenever I was playing with Irini, Billy wanted to join in, but I never allowed him to. He would argue with me and make jokes that I could tell were at my expense but that I couldn't really understand. Tusiime and Billy shared a room, and they got along with each other.

Abigail and Irini got along really well. Abigail used to do gymnastics and would teach some of the moves to Irini. We barely saw our other foster sister, Gabrielle, but she was cool with everyone when we did.

The one thing that I really loved about the Smiths was that family meant everything to them. Sunday was a family day, and every Sunday they would visit Arnie's parents or other family members would come to their house.

· · ·

I could not wait to start school. I was so eager to finally start on the journey that I'd spent years praying for, but I worried I would not do well. I had no doubt that my siblings were going to do great in school. Back in the refugee camp, they did very well, whereas I kept failing, never paying attention in class. My job was to fight kids to protect my siblings, and I was good at that. I didn't want to be the bully here. I didn't believe or have confidence in myself, and I did not know who I was. I made a promise that I would not show anyone these things until I had found myself.

Before we started school, we had to get vaccinated, seven shots all at once. I could not move my arms that day. My siblings were all crying. Finally, two weeks after arriving in America, we started school. Tusiime went to middle school with me, but Irini had to face elementary school, and Zawadi high school, on their own.

My first day of eighth grade was very interesting. The school was so big. Most people were white, and I only saw about five Black kids. I did not really talk; all I did was watch and try to learn. The best thing I did was smile at my classmates. I was telling them, "I see you. I hear you. I cannot understand you, but I am friendly and willing to learn."

In most of my classes, my classmates stared at me, but I was always looking at the teacher. I couldn't understand what the teacher was saying, but I understood it when she used the whiteboard to explain things. All my teachers were women, which made it easy for me to connect with them. My language arts teacher did not really help me that much. She always gave me things to do by myself, but I could not really understand any of the papers she gave me. Not only did I not yet know English, but many of the topics of study at school were different than what I'd learned about in Uganda.

Luckily, I had kids who were willing to help and be my friend, even when I did not speak the language they spoke. That made me feel welcomed. I did not really fit in, but that was not the goal; the goal was to get an education. I was on a mission to find myself and to make sure I became the person I was meant to be. I did not care if people liked me or not, or if they said mean things to my face that I did not understand. That was not my problem, that was their problem. I had to find my key and unlock the potential of the woman inside me I knew I could become.

My brother and I had different lunchtimes, so I usually ate lunch alone. Tusiime always fit in everywhere he went. He was so welcoming. Being a boy made it easy for him to get along with the other guys.

I guess the stereotype that Black men are good at sports also helped him. Girls were always all over him. Some girls, when they found out that he was my brother, tried to be friends with me, but I hated that. All I did was smile at them and walk away.

School became my life. I went to school from 6 a.m. to 6 p.m. every day because teachers came early and stayed late to tutor me after our foster parents asked them to help. Before that, Arnie and Ilene would stay up until midnight each night helping us learn. That became another motivation for me: knowing that there were all these people who truly wanted to see me succeed. I loved school with all my heart. I became the cool nerd. I hated getting Bs and always wanted As. If I didn't get 100 percent on my exams and was given a chance to retake it, I would retake it.

I was always thinking of my future: how I wanted my life to play out and how I wanted my future kids to look up to me. I recognized that the education I was gaining and the opportunities I was given would not only help me, but also others in the future, like women and youth from my home. It was no longer just about me. And that pushed me and kept me going.

. . .

After we started school, our foster parents drove us on the weekends to visit Tibasima, Badulu, and Alfred at their apartment in a different suburb. I was excited to see them and see how their new life was going and find out things like what American food they liked or hated.

The apartment where they were living was in a nearby suburb. It was in a very nice complex that was surrounded by trees with a basketball court in the back. Other refugees in the complex who had been here for a while helped Tibasima and my brothers navigate both the area and the American lifestyle.

America was fun, strange, and hard. So many things weren't what I'd envisioned in my mind. To me, America was all like New York City—no grass, all buildings and concrete and bright lights that twinkled like Christmas every night. When we first arrived in Utah, the cities seemed so small compared to Kampala I thought they were just villages, and I was surprised by all of the open fields.

So many things struck me as different or unusual besides cheese pizza and garage doors. I knew nothing of dishwashers, and the first morning at the Smiths' home, I went to the kitchen and started washing dishes by hand until they stopped me and showed me that a machine could do it. People dress casually here. Congolese are known to dress well and be the best dancers, so to me dressing casually came across as sloppy. And in summer, how short girls' shorts are was shocking to me, because at home everyone wears something long to cover their legs. I knew very little about the Internet—Tibasima was on Facebook, but Google, YouTube, and other social media were new to me. I was amazed at how many young kids had phones—I didn't have my first phone until I was eighteen.

But school was really different. Not just little things, like learning to use a locker—I hated that; it took me until ninth grade to figure out how to work the combination lock. Or that here I could braid my hair—most Ugandan schools require Black girls to keep their hair very short, no longer than half a centimeter, because the schools think that long hair is distracting. Or that everyone spoke a different language than me, although at least it was just one different language. Back at the refugee camp, the refugees and teachers all came from so many different regions, and we all had a different first language—my family's native tongue is Kihema, and we also speak Luganda and Swahili. But even second languages were different in the camp—in Congo, many children learn French (my older brothers did, but I was too young when we lived in Congo), but many of the teachers knew English as their second language. All of that made learning harder since someone always had to translate something to someone else.

But the learning style was also very different. It wasn't easy to learn in the refugee camp since there were hundreds of kids jammed together with just a few teachers. Here, the classes seemed small. And no one beat you if you were late to class!

The teachers here really seemed to care, and they also had better materials to teach with. I really liked the teaching style—at home we just took notes and took two big exams a year, that's it. No quizzes, no practice as you go. Just memorize everything you can and hope you pass the test. But here, things were hands-on, like having lab projects to really understand the science we were learning.

The biggest difference was our motivation. Here, you learn for your future. There, girls had no idea what their future held—when they'd be married and have to leave school. There, the goal was just to teach the basics of reading, writing, and math, and the motivation was to avoid the pain of a beating if you got it wrong. Here, the goal is to create your life.

10

CHRISTMAS CULTURE CLASH

OUR FIRST CHRISTMAS WITH THE SMITHS was not what I expected, and definitely not how we celebrate back home. In Uganda, we buy new clothes that we save to wear to church to celebrate Christmas Day. Some people only go to church that one day of the year, just so they can show off their new outfit.

Growing up, Christmas and New Year's were the best days. I have always looked forward to them, because those are the days we eat good food, play music, and dance. Christmas is the only day of the year that we get to eat rice and beef and drink soda.

About two months after we'd arrived in the US, Christmas was getting close, and we saw Ilene buying gifts and wrapping them up. I was confused until the Smiths explained how they celebrate Christmas. I was very shocked, but I went along with everything. The gifts kept arriving. She mostly did her shopping when we were at school, but if some arrived when we were home, she would quickly hide them. Ilene asked us what we wanted. Irini and Tusiime said they wanted bikes. Zawadi and I always said, "Whatever you get us, we will be grateful."

All the kids in the family got to buy each other gifts. We wrote all the siblings' names on paper, and then we put them in a bowl. We shook them and mixed them up, and then each child drew a name. Whichever name you got was the person you were buying a gift for.

On Christmas Eve, we went out to dinner, then all sat in the living room and opened gifts. Gabrielle had drawn my name, and she gave me a fluffy pink robe, a black sweater, a pink sweater, a fluffy set of pajamas, and four packs of gum. I always used to ask her if she had gum—I would not go a day without chewing gum. And back then, I loved pink so much and wore pink clothes all the time. I still love fluffy things. I enjoyed that night, but in the back of my mind, I still imagined how people back home were celebrating, with music playing everywhere and people just having fun.

We had to go to bed early. That night when we were sleeping, our foster parents brought down all the presents they'd kept hidden and put them under the tree. On Christmas morning, we were supposed to come down in our pajamas, but I woke up so early that I took a shower and got ready. I don't remember why I did that, but I felt more comfortable that way. I remember when we got called downstairs, Billy and I met by the bathroom door. Billy just stared at me for a moment and said, "So you got ready."

"Yep," I said. Billy looked confused. Sometimes what I did never really made sense to him.

All of us went downstairs, and Ilene videoed us opening presents. Everyone was so happy. I was excited, but I did not show it. I did not know how to express myself sometimes, and most of the time I came off as mean, even if I didn't intend to.

I will never forget the camera and electric blanket the Smiths gave me that first Christmas. These two things brought so much joy to me, and I still have them. On the weekends, I would get in different outfits and take pictures. My siblings got annoyed by me always asking them to take photos of me. I would take my camera to school sometimes to take photos with my friends and teachers. My electric blanket made the cold Utah weather more bearable—I put the temperature up all the way to high every night, and I slept so well. But what I found unusual was that they always gave us socks as gifts. I never really got the point of that.

On that first Christmas day, it snowed, and I found out how close-minded I can be. We all played outside in the snow, but I got so mad when Billy hit me with a snowball that I went back in and up to bed. I watched everyone else play through the window and heard Ilene ask Billy why he did that.

In the evening, we got ready to go visit Tibasima and my brothers. I took photos of all the things I got for Christmas to show them. When I told Ilene, she nearly died laughing. Then she told everyone, and they all laughed. At that point, I did not know if I should laugh with them or be mad.

I was such a serious person, so closed-off and close-minded. I did not understand jokes or like them. I never showed my emotions, just my mean words, and saw people become scared of me. I hated getting close to people. Getting close to people meant they would walk away or hurt me. The only people who really understood me were Tusiime, Zawadi, and Irini. So I laughed with the Smiths, because I did not want to destroy a fun moment like I always seemed to do.

We got dropped off at Tibasima's place. We found my family cooking and watching a movie in the little apartment. They did not go anywhere. At night, we got to talk with people back home. We told them how we missed Christmas over there. Then we put on music and started dancing, and it was so much fun.

After thirty minutes of dancing, we heard a knock on the door. My brother opened the door and saw the police. The old woman who lived downstairs did not really like my brother and Tibasima. She always called the police on them for the littlest things. I got so scared. The police officer stood in the doorway as he took notes and my brothers' names. He asked us to keep it down.

My brothers were friends with a guy called Bobby who lived in the complex, and he was often around when we were there. Bobby was very kind. He had three dogs, and he loved that Irini played with them. Every weekend when we went to visit our family, we always visited him too. He always teased me that I could fight him. He said I looked tough, and that he wanted to see who was the toughest, me or him.

One day when we were all coming down the stairs to walk Bobby back to his apartment, talking as we went, the old woman stood in her doorway and started yelling at us. Bobby told her if he ever heard again that she called the police on my family, he would call them back on her or file a report of harassment.

"Your dog barks all night. Have you ever seen them call the police to tell you to keep your dog quiet?" he said.

She went back inside, and she never called the police again, no matter how loud the music was.

//

THE BATTLE FOR US BEGINS

IN JANUARY, SOMEONE—I DON'T KNOW WHO—had the idea for the local news to interview us on TV and explain our story. Arnie and Ilene asked us if we wanted to be on TV, and we said yes. Of course, as kids, we were so excited by the thought. I called my brothers and Tibasima to explain everything to them. They didn't like the idea and told us to say no, but we did the news segment anyway. On a cheerful but chilly day, we got excused from school and met a camera crew and the interviewer at our home. Ilene told all the neighbors we were going to be on TV, and everyone promised to watch.

The first weekend we visited Tibasima and my brothers after the interview aired, we got a full-blown African-style lecture from Tibasima. First when we got there, then during dinner, then she lectured us again as we were leaving on Sunday evening.

"Do not think you have gotten to heaven. This is just another country. Do not think because you are here in America, you cannot get beaten," she said. "Those people are just using you for money. Do not think they truly love you."

By the time we left, it was just too much. Tibasima and my brothers just hated the idea of us being on TV. I kind of understood them, but at the same time I did not. I thought they were just trying to protect us from the world.

I hated how people felt sorry for us after the news segment aired, but I didn't dwell on it. I focused all of my energy on finding myself and my purpose and building up my confidence. I did not have time for those who felt sorry for me or did not like me.

That interview severed all goodwill between our foster parents and Tibasima and my brothers. Tibasima complained to our caseworker, Emma, that no one had asked for her permission. From then on, Tibasima was rude to Arnie and Ilene when they dropped us off and picked us up. It got so bad that Emma suggested we start taking the train and bus to visit Tibasima and my brothers.

Tibasima's new friends in America who were refugees themselves had already been advising her to ask for custody of us. I had mixed feelings about the idea.

"We don't want you to lose your culture," Tibasima said.

She shared more reasons, but culture kept coming up over and over. There is some truth to this, and I did think that if I lived with Tibasima, it would be easier to talk with family and friends back home, but I knew the main reason was money. If Tibasima and my brothers became our foster parents, they would get money from the agency that would pay for the bills.

When we first came to the US, we didn't really get along with a lot of people in the faith-based agency that ran the foster care program we were part of, and at first we did not see eye to eye with Emma. When we asked the agency to allow us to live with Tibasima, they told her to take classes to learn how to become a parent. I was so mad that they expected her to go take parenting classes while she was already trying to learn English.

It always felt like they saw us as a problem. It felt like we gave them headaches when we tried to express ourselves. We told them where we stood. We were very clear, and I was not scared to speak up when it was needed. The people in the agency did not really understand what it meant to completely leave your country and then be separated from the only people you knew in your new country. When we had to explain that we had been through so much with our family, and that's why we needed to be with them, I felt like no one understood. We did not even know English well enough to explain so that they could understand. But also, no one tried to put themselves in our shoes.

Every month, we went to family court and a judge would determine whether our foster family was doing a good job and we were being good kids. Tibasima told us that when we went to court, we needed to tell the judge we wanted to live with our family, and so we did. She also told us that we needed to cry.

I really hated court days. We hurt our foster family, especially Ilene, when we would tell the judge that we wanted to live with Tibasima, and I hated hurting them. The Smiths took all four of us, we didn't want to be separated, and cooked for us, treated us like their own children, and loved us. I hated the bad energy that we brought home from court. I hated it all.

After listening to Tibasima say that the Smiths only took us in for the money, I decided I was going to make them work for it. Sometimes when they picked us up from Tibasima's house, we would act mad to show them that we wanted to stay with our family.

I gave them a hard time at home because sometimes it felt like they did not care. I think I was the one child whose actions and words hurt my foster mom the most. I did not see the effort she put into things. When I say I was a very closed-off person and close-minded, trust me, because I was. People's effort and words meant nothing to me. For example, Ilene cooked dinner, and when we sat down to eat, everyone would try the food except me. I would just say I didn't like it without even trying it.

Some things I did on purpose, but most of the time, I was just trying to figure myself out. They blamed me for everything that my siblings did, who would say I told them to do things, just like Tibasima had always blamed me. I just had to tell myself it is what it is.

This all made the energy change, and not in a good way. I feel like back then, the only thing I did right was to do well in school. Everything else I did was wrong. I did not know how to talk to other people. The only people I knew how to love were my siblings.

I never really considered other people's feelings. My delivery was really bad. Most of the time, I would say things and Ilene would understand them in a different way than I intended. I would get so frustrated trying to get my words right that I would end up just going quiet, and Ilene would have to try to figure me out on her own.

I guess I never really tried to put myself in other people's shoes, either.

12

FORCED THERAPY FAILS

WE HAVE A PRETTY DARK SENSE OF HUMOR IN AFRICA. It's one way we deal with difficult lives. But I learned the hard way that there are some words no one jokes about in America.

In the Smiths' house, we ate dinner around 6–7 p.m., sometimes even earlier. After dinner, we would all go to bed. I couldn't get used to the schedule. Usually by 10 p.m., I was hungry again. I would go into Ilene's room and ask her to cook eggs or make me something to eat, and she always said yes. In the Smiths' kitchen, there was a whiteboard where we wrote notes, like shopping lists and reminders and sometimes just something cute or funny. When Ilene went to bed after making these late-night meals for me, I would leave a message on the whiteboard before going back upstairs to my bed. I'd leave things like: *I want to kill myself because I am not living with Tibasima.* Or: *I just want to die. I am tired of this world.*

I grew up speaking words like these. To an African parent, when you say something like that, they would tell you, "Go kill yourself and see if we cannot live without you." African parents answer you back with their own joke, their way of saying they know you're just using dark humor to blow off steam. The way I grew up, no one talked about depression or mental health. People were just supposed to toughen up and figure life out. Looking back, I think people didn't really know how to talk about mental health. I see the same issue sometimes here in America, that there is still a stigma around mental health, and especially for Black people.

When I started writing on the whiteboard, the Smiths did not know exactly who it was, but they guessed it was me, probably because I was the last in the kitchen. One day, as I was writing a dark message, Billy hid and watched me until I finished writing. He thought I didn't see him, but I knew he was there. When I finished writing, Billy came out of hiding to read what I wrote. Billy's face looked like he was so scared. He took the whiteboard to his parents' room.

The next day our caseworker Emma was at our home after school, telling my siblings and me that we were going to start therapy. I did not know what therapy was, so I asked her. She said I was going to talk to someone who would help me with my problems.

"What problems?" I asked.

She told me I would see.

"I don't have problems," I said. "I am in school. You have solved all my problems by putting me in school."

She did not really understand what I said because my English back then was very broken. I got mad and was done talking. She tried to ask questions to try to understand, but all I would say was, "It okay, it okay."

That was my response whenever people in America didn't understand me. Sometimes when I did this, my siblings would start laughing because they knew "it okay" meant I was done talking no matter how hard anyone pushed me. I always tried my best to never disrespect the therapist or my foster parents. I would rather keep saying "it okay" for hours than be disrespectful to any of them.

The next day, we started therapy. The therapist was a woman with red hair—that was surprising to me since I hadn't seen many redheads at that point. She came to our home after school, and we would sit in the Smiths' home office for the therapy sessions. For the first session, I got off school early, so I was the first one to meet with her.

She introduced herself; she held a bunch of white papers in her hands. I smiled at her, but I was not otherwise very friendly to her. She asked me to introduce myself.

I said, "I am Desange!"

Then she started asking me questions.

"What do you like to do in your free time?"

"School," I said.

And the questions kept coming. More and more, and I got to the point where I was so annoyed by her questions. Instead of answering them, I just stared at her, right in her eyes. I told her I did not want to answer these questions anymore.

"You want to take a break?" she asked.

"Okay," I said.

When I got back from the break, I asked when we would be done.

"After we finish playing this game," she said and began to explain how it worked. "We will play while I ask questions."

"We play the game or we do the questions, you choose," I told her.

"We can do both," she replied.

I got up from the floor where we were sitting, and I sat on the chair. She kept talking to me, but I would not reply. Finally, she gave up and said, "You are done."

I hated it the whole time. She was asking about my feelings and giving me examples of situations to respond to, and I did not like any of it! In my head I thought, *I spent the whole day at school, and then I come home, and I get another lecture.* I was finished with being lectured at home the moment I stopped living with Tibasima.

The therapist met with all my siblings. That night when we went to bed, we sisters called Tusiime to our room to talk.

I asked them, "What do you think? Did you guys answer the questions?"

They all looked at me and asked at the same time, "Did you answer them?"

"No," I said.

They told me they did answer a few questions but hated it the whole time. I asked them if they played the game, and they said no.

The second day, the therapist came without any questions, and we just had a normal conversation. She asked about my culture back home—those are the types of questions I was willing to answer because people usually have the wrong idea about Africa. I did give her one piece of personal information.

"Yesterday you asked me what I love doing," I said to her. "I love dancing more than anything."

And that was it. We closed our session.

After her sessions that day with all of us, the therapist stayed and talked with Ilene for thirty minutes. I have always thought the therapist shared what we told her with Ilene, and I did not like that.

We had therapy every week, and from then on, I would not say anything for most of the sessions. I just looked at the therapist. Or sometimes I would just look down, but then I would remember that in America, if you look down you are disrespecting those older than you. I would look her in the eyes.

She would ask if she had done something wrong. She would ask about my day and school. If I didn't want to answer a question, I would say I did not know. Sometimes she would say, "I will give you this if you talk." I would make sure the item would be worth the price of my words. For example, I loved photography and had so many pictures I'd taken. I wanted a photo album for them. She brought one to a session and said I could have it if I told her something about the refugee camp.

I said, "Life in the refugee camp was tough. They burned our house down." When I wouldn't say any more, she said I hadn't said enough to earn the photo album. I reminded her that she promised, and then she reluctantly handed it over.

I hated therapy with all my heart. I didn't hate the therapist herself, I hated the fact that she asked about my feelings. I did not grow up expressing myself or talking about myself. Back then my emotional walls were built up sky high. Trusting someone—anyone—was out of the question, but I particularly did not trust the therapist because I was certain what we told her she then told Ilene. My siblings and I always wondered why the therapist would always stay after the sessions and talk with Ilene for so long, sometimes for hours.

I only trusted myself, my siblings, and some of the Smith family. Sometimes I would consider talking to Arnie, but I knew he was one with Ilene; he couldn't hide things from her. I did not trust the organization that ran our foster care program—in fact, I hated it. It felt like they controlled everything. We couldn't sleep over at a friend's house without asking our foster parents to ask the foster care program to ask the judge if it was okay. We lost the chance to go on church youth trips and camping trips because it took two to four weeks for us to get an answer from the judge on whether we could go, and by then it was too late. So we just stopped asking to travel or stay the night anywhere.

The people we encountered who worked with the foster care program did not seem to understand our point of view. I felt confused and like everyone was against us. I decided to keep everything I was feeling inside, because there was no one that I could open up to, no one that I trusted to keep my words to themselves.

During this time all I needed was to just be heard, but it felt like no one knew the right way to listen. It felt like the people who were supposed to help me and protect me didn't have my best interests at heart and disregarded what I had to say.

Looking back, maybe part of the problem was that no one liked the way I was sharing. I struggled with the delivery of my words—sometimes I would say something that people took the wrong way even though I tried to say it in a good way.

It felt like people hated me more than my siblings because I always said what was on my mind. I do not know how to hide what I feel; if I am mad, I will show you that I am mad. I am not the kind of person who will sit back and watch you do something wrong and keep quiet. I speak up.

Being vulnerable with someone was something that I could not do then, not even with my siblings. It has been an immense journey for me to learn how to express myself in a way that helps me build relationships and heal.

13

CONGO KIDS, STEP OUT

WHILE LIVING WITH THE SMITHS, we were always saying we wanted to go and live with our family. The Smiths and the foster care program did not understand why; I think they thought we were being a pain about it. Even at the time, I understood that we were not the easiest kids to deal with. I could tell we brought stress to the Smith home. Sometimes I could see their point of view, but other times I couldn't.

There was a time when we came home later than usual on a Sunday evening after a weekend at Tibasima's house. After that happened for the third time, Ilene said we could no longer go to Tibasima's early on Fridays.

I did not see what one had to do with the other, and I really couldn't understand what the problem was. The latest we ever came home was about 8:30 p.m., plenty of time before our 10 p.m. bedtime. I wondered if maybe Ilene wanted to spend more time with us, but that did not seem to be the reason. I did not say anything, but I thought, *I am here all week, and the weekends are the only days that I spend with my family*. The whole situation was a red flag for me. I felt like I was being attacked for trying to spend more time with my family.

But in other ways, Ilene's feelings were easy for me to understand, especially after our monthly hearings in family court that were part of our foster care arrangement, where I'd always have to follow Tibasima's instructions and tell the judge I wanted to go live with my family even though I still wasn't sure what I really wanted. I hated court days— like when we came home from weekend visits to my family, everyone's emotions ran high those days.

It was so painful to me. I didn't really want to leave the Smiths at that time. One day, it just became too much. I cried in court as I told the judge we wanted to live with our family. Ilene was very sad. When we got back home, she went straight to her room. A little while later, I went to find her because I needed something—exactly what, I don't recall now. She was not in her room, and I called out for her.

"Yes, honey?" she replied from the bathroom. It sounded like she was in the bath, and I could tell she was crying. We talked about whatever little thing I needed, and I was about to leave the room when she called my name.

"Yes, Mom?"

"Are you unhappy with our family?"

"No."

"Why do you always tell the judge you want to live with your family?"

I did not want to answer. At the end of the day, I was just doing what I was told by Tibasima. I wanted to stay, and I, too, was in so much pain to hurt Ilene this way, but I couldn't show it. How could I? Emotions were hard for me to express anyway, and I was afraid any emotion I showed, anything different I said, would get Tibasima in trouble and cause so much difficulty for everyone.

"We do everything we can," she said. "We take you guys to the swimming pool, and we have fun with you guys. We do things for you guys that other foster parents would not do for other kids."

I said nothing. I just waited, still listening. Even if I knew what to say or what would be okay, I was raised to never respond back to someone older than you; when they were talking, you listened.

"You guys make our family look bad! Like we treat you guys in the wrong way."

I did not know what to say to her. If I had the right words to say, I would have said them. I could hear her tears and the pain in her voice as she tried to figure out where they went wrong with us.

When there was no more to say, I went straight to the bedroom I shared with my sisters. I thought that Ilene thought we did not appreciate her and her family for what they had done for us. I felt like they expected us to be different, that somehow we didn't live up to their expectations. I was sad. I hated the fact that we were hurting someone by trying to go live with our family. At the end of the day, the Smiths were very nice to us and did everything for us they could. Ilene treated us the same as her own kids, waking up every morning to take us to school and making dinner for us. They knew how important education was to us and supported us in school and showed up to every activity that we had. We had our disagreements and our different points of view, but that does not take away the fact that they were good people who sacrificed a lot to let us in their home.

. . .

By the spring of 2015, we had been living with the Smiths for about six months, and it seemed that things kept happening that made me feel so uncomfortable. At first, it was little things. For example, the

Smiths gave us each a journal to write our private thoughts in, which I enjoyed doing. I always kept mine under my pillow. One day I came home from school and found it sitting out in plain sight, and I wondered who'd been reading it.

Before we left for America, we'd been coached by Kahi to never touch money that was left lying around, even if it was a trivial amount. It could be a test to see if we would steal. The Smiths had a piano in their home office that we enjoyed playing, and one day, some money was left on top of the piano. I saw it and, sure it was a test, warned my siblings not to touch it.

And then there were lots of little moments when they knew we had done something, and we couldn't figure out how they knew. Most kids go through those feelings in any home, but we were convinced we were being spied on because back in Africa we'd been warned that people in America had cameras everywhere and were always watching you. We siblings came up with a lot of theories of where cameras could be hiding in the Smith home. There was a smoke detector in our room, and its cover didn't close completely. We were sure that was because a camera was hiding inside.

Our birthday was another awkward moment. All of us siblings celebrated our birthdays together on January 1, a common custom for refugees like us that don't have birth records. The Smiths threw a party for us and invited Tibasima and our brothers to come across town to their home for the party. They also gave us birthday money. They were trying to do something nice. But because of the party, we didn't get the weekend away with our family, which is something we cherished.

Since we typically went to church with Tibasima, that Sunday, being at the Smiths' home, we decided to sleep in. The Smiths were upset and hurt that after providing the party and giving us birthday money, we chose not to go to church with them. But that made all they'd done for our birthday not feel like a gift at all, but more like a bribe. The Smiths demanded to know whose idea it was for us to skip church. None of us siblings answered, and so they assumed it was my idea. Yet again, I was blamed since I'm known as the outspoken one, the ringleader, regardless of what I or my siblings really do.

Then, that spring, the Smith family got a dog—exactly what kind, I don't know, but it looked similar to a black lab. I do not like dogs, and back then, I was truly scared of them. Where I come from, dogs are trained to be fierce and are used for protection. The last thing I wanted to do was to live with a dog.

But one day after school, I came home to find there was a dog in the house. When I saw it, I went straight to my bed upstairs. Whenever the dog tried to come to me, I would run away. I spent the whole evening in my room. Ilene had to put the dog in a separate room for me to come eat dinner. I did not feel safe anymore in the house that I slept in.

Maybe they got the dog to find more happiness. Abigail loved to play with it, and the dog seemed to make all the Smiths happy, unlike my siblings and me. It felt like since we came into the Smiths' lives, we'd taken away their peace and happiness.

Their getting the dog felt like a slap in the face to me. I felt betrayed, like I was being told it was time for me to leave. I told myself it was now okay for the judge to tell me to go live with Tibasima, since it seemed I no longer mattered at the Smiths' home.

One night I knelt on the floor to pray, and tears poured out of me, but no words could come out of my mouth. I felt like I was no longer a person, just a ball that would be kicked around. Did Tibasima want us to come to her for the money, or did she really want us to return to her arms to be a real family? The Smiths were kind in their way, and seemed to want the best for us, but did they really want *us* with them, the *real* us?

It got to the point where it seemed like the Smiths were just stuck with us. Getting a dog, getting mad at us for coming home late from visiting Tibasima, and creating rules about when we could see our family made the Smith house feel like a prison, not a home. The foster care program was already hard enough on us with all of their rules about where we could go and what we could do. We didn't need our foster parents adding more.

Even though I had been saying in the monthly court hearings that I wanted to live with Tibasima, I had just been doing what Tibasima told me to do. Up until this point, in my heart I was against the idea of leaving the Smiths, even when some of my siblings were for it. I choose to see the good in people and to try to understand that no one is perfect. I even tried to come up with ways to live under the same roof as the dog. But then the Smiths did something that hurt me very much and made me decide I was wrong to want to try to stay with them.

Gabrielle, the Smiths' daughter who was in her twenties, got married. We were all at the wedding, doing the wedding photos outside of the wedding venue. We first took a photo with everyone involved with the wedding, and then one with just the family only.

After the big family photo, Ilene said, "Congo kids, step out." She meant now it was time for her and the *main* family to take photos. She said this in front of everyone, and I felt so embarrassed. Many times they told us we were a part of their family and that we were their kids. But then they took family photos of the wedding of someone we were supposed to see as our sister, and we were excluded. Their words and actions did not match.

At the reception after the wedding, my siblings and I served food to the guests. Billy helped here and there, but mostly we did the work. My sisters and I wore matching skirts and tops that Ilene had bought for us, and I wondered if she did that so we could be identified as the waitresses.

At home that night, my siblings and I talked about what happened. My emotions were all over the place. Zawadi said to me, "I told you." She'd never believed the Smiths truly saw us as part of their family. I felt like maybe it was time to do what Tibasima had been telling us to do for so long—maybe we should run away. So, we planned an escape.

Running away wasn't my idea, and the way we did it wasn't even my plan. Tibasima always told us to just leave without warning, take the train since we already knew how to do that, go downtown, call the police, and tell them we wanted to go live with her. That was all her plan, but I was the one that decided to put it into action. We waited for a couple days, all the while worried about those hidden cameras we were sure the Smiths had planted to watch us. Then one day in the middle of the week, I told my siblings that after school that day, Zawadi, Tusiime, and I were leaving. Irini was too young to go.

After school, Zawadi walked to the station, and Tusiime and I met her there. It was sunny out but still pretty chilly—I was still getting used to the idea that it could be cold when the sun was shining. I was wearing a pink hoodie—my signature color then—and black jeans. As much as we laughed on the train on our way there, pretending everything was going to be okay, I was very scared. I did not know how it was all going to end, but deep down, I knew our lives were about to take a big curve, but to where, I did not know. But I knew that by running away, we could not go back to the Smiths.

We rode the train all the way to downtown, then we got off and called the police. Zawadi had coins with her to use for a pay phone. She put them down when we realized that 911 calls were free. I grabbed them and kept them, and Zawadi teased me.

"They're going to take you to prison for taking those coins," Zawadi said, and Tusiime and I started laughing. Sometimes, when things are tense, you just need to laugh.

The police arrived in about five minutes. We explained why we called and what was going on. We told them we needed to go live with Tibasima and that we had been telling the foster care program, but that they were not listening to us. We said the family we were living with was just too strict, but we explained that they were good people.

We thought the police could help us. We didn't understand how the system works.

At that time, our English still wasn't very good, but the two police officers were able to look us up in the system and figure out where we belonged. They took us to the foster program office. I felt like I was a piece of property and that the only question they wanted to consider was: Who did I belong to? I didn't feel like they saw me as a human being with my own feelings, questions, and needs. The same fear I had in Uganda, when my future was so uncertain, returned. In the foster care program, I was now labeled as bad, as the ringleader, the rebellious one in my family.

We sat in the office of the foster care program manager, who was at her desk. Ilene and Arnie came in. Ilene was crying, her eyes were red, and when they sat down, she cradled her head in her arms folded on top of the desk.

"Do you know what this means?" Ilene asked us.

"Yes," we said.

"You are not going to be living with us anymore," she said.

My siblings and I said okay, acting like we did not care.

That hurt her and she cried harder. I did not feel empathy at that moment, I was too angry.

I had a book in my hand that I was reading for a school project. With a voice full of anger she said, "Give me back my book!"

I gave it to her. I also had a water bottle that was not mine, so I thrust it at her and said, "Here is your water bottle, too."

She grabbed it and just walked out of the office crying. Arnie stayed back. He was very sad. He had been quiet, but now said, "I am so sorry this is happening."

He asked us for hugs before he left, and we did give him hugs goodbye.

It was the start of a new journey for us. We didn't know what would happen next. Once again, the unknown was so scary.

14

EVERY ACTION HAS CONSEQUENCES

WE HAD DONE IT. WE HAD RUN AWAY. And now it was time for us to face the consequences. Because no matter how young you are, there are always consequences. And ours was that we did not get to be together under one roof for a while. I had to say goodbye to Tusiime and Zawadi, which was so hard after already having said goodbye to Irini. No one family could take three kids in at the last minute—there were few that could take so many in general—and so we all got different temporary homes in different towns while they were looking for permanent homes for us. Zawadi and Tusiime went to nearby suburbs. I went to what felt like the middle of nowhere, like they wanted me far from trains or other means of escape.

Arnie, Abigail, Billy, and Gabrielle brought us a few changes of clothes at a gas station where we were meeting the people who would drive us to our different places to stay. Everyone but Arnie was so mad at us. I understood, we were hurting their mom and their family. I never expected them to understand our situation. The kids just stood outside the car and did not look us in the face. Arnie said, "Just remember we love you."

I thought, *You meant to say, "I love you," not "we."* Because I did not believe any of the other Smiths felt that way.

A woman picked me up in a very small red car. All I had with me besides the clothes the Smiths brought was my school backpack and my Bible. It was night, we drove for hours, and I wondered where she was taking me. Part of our journey took us through a narrow road and onto a bridge that was so tiny and very scary; I thought it would be my last night on earth. Eventually, I fell asleep. She woke me up when we arrived. It was very dark outside, and all I could see was that I was surrounded by mountains.

I met the family that I would be temporarily staying with plus another girl from foster care who was living there. She and I shared a room. I went straight to bed, but I couldn't sleep that night. I started thinking about my life, and I was so scared. During the first months that I was living here in America, I never really lived in the present; I was always in the future or past. That night I thought my future was doomed, that we had ruined everything—that the people who ran the foster care program must have been madder at me than any of my siblings, and that's why they shipped me off, far away from them.

I kept worrying about how Tusiime and Zawadi were, asking myself if they were okay, like I was their mother. And I wondered if they even worried about me. Then I realized I would miss school, and there was nothing I hated more than for anything to stand in my way of going to school.

Eventually, I knelt on the floor and cried while I prayed. I felt like I was a failure, and that no one, especially the people in the foster care program, understood us. I felt so lonely. These were my prayers that night:

Dear Lord, God, I am trusting you. I am putting my life in your hands, Lord. You brought us all the way from Africa to America. I know you must have a plan, Lord. Please, Lord, do not forsake me and my siblings. Lord, we may be separated from each other, please choose the right families for us. Lord, help Tibasima and Badulu to be foster parents fast, and let this be the last time I move. Lord, I cannot live like this, knowing that anytime I could be moved!

Lord, I trust you and I know you have a good plan for my siblings and me. I beg you, Lord, to protect them for me. Lead them and show them what to do. I trust you and I believe you will come through for us. Amen.

That was the longest night I'd had in a very long time. I wanted someone to tell me it would be okay. I went over a lifetime of memories in my mind, thinking about some of the worst things we'd endured. I decided I needed to be strong. After all, if we survived our house literally burning down in Uganda, we could survive metaphorically burning down our home with the Smiths. I had to look at it as another challenge that I had to face. Problems are challenges that we must overcome to stay on our path. What would life be without struggles? They are what make life so interesting.

I started thinking about the Smith family, what they must be going through, especially Ilene. I tried to put myself in her shoes. What would I have done? Probably the same thing: let the kids go before anything bad happened to them while trying to run away. But I still could not understand why they told us we were family and then did not act like it.

I believe that what hurt Ilene most was her expectations. The Smiths expected us to live with them until we were twenty-one years old, because that was the plan Tibasima agreed to when she signed the agreement with the foster care program. But the plan changed. Whenever the Smiths asked my siblings and me if we would live with them until we were twenty-one years old, my siblings always said yes, but I always smiled but never really answered the question. Not because I did not want to live with them, but because I did not want to say words that I could not stand by.

Finally, I fell asleep that night, holding my Bible in my arms.

. . .

I woke up in the morning to a cat staring at me. I screamed. I was so scared. I believed like many Africans that witches enter cats and use them to do their dirty work.

The cat ran away, I prayed, then I just stayed in bed. The girl I shared a room with kept coming into the room. She had short hair and cuts on her arms.

Finally, she said, "Aren't you getting up today?"

I said, "Good morning, what is your name?"

She told me, and then said, "They need you out of the room. We are going to do chores."

I said okay and did my morning routine, then went outside. She was very quiet and did not really talk much. I asked her what the name of the town was and why it was not close to anything. She replied that she didn't know. It was kind of chilly outside, so we went back to our room.

"So what is your story?" I asked her.

She said it was complicated, and she talked about her parents, but I could tell she was so lonely and that she thought there was no point to this life.

"What is your story?" she asked me.

"I am just another refugee girl trying to make it in this world," I replied.

"Do you have any siblings?"

"Yes, but we are separated."

"Same," she said.

At least we had something to connect us.

"Why were you crying last night?" she said.

"I guess it is karma doing its work. The last family I left, my actions made someone cry. The tears were returning the pain, I guess."

"So you believe in the Bible?" she asked.

"Yes. Without God I don't think I would be where I am," I said.

"Where you are in pain, you mean," she said.

"I mean in life, you know. I am from a different continent and life there was not too good to me."

"Well, I hope your God sees you through, because my God ran away from me a long time ago," she said.

"He will see me through; this here is nothing. God has brought me far! I try to remember we have to go through challenges in life to grow. Even Jesus went through problems when He came here on earth. Who are we human beings, thinking we will not go through problems? Do you want to try my God? We can always pray together and read the Bible together."

"Yes," she said.

I did not know if she said yes to just be nice or if she really wanted to believe. "You have to believe with all your heart and have no doubts," I told her.

"Yes," she said.

My English back then was not that good, but I did try my best to explain the Bible. It felt nice to know that I was not in this alone. We prayed together; for those few weeks, we did everything together.

The family I was staying with was nice. I became friends with their daughter who was still in high school and living at home; they had other adult children who were married and had moved away.

One day I asked to call Ilene. I talked to her, and I apologized. As much as I wanted to tell her that running away had been Tibasima's idea, not mine, I knew it wouldn't matter. I knew they blamed me for everything, and I was already used to being blamed for other people's mistakes. And so, I let it be.

I asked her if she could take me back in, and she cried as she said no. I cried, too. She said Irini could stay and Zawadi could come back to live with her if she wanted. To me, that was unbelievable, but then, I realized she saw Zawadi as the easy one. I was the troublemaker, at least that was how my personality came across. They thought I was the one telling my siblings things to do. I felt unwanted and decided I was glad I left, because at the end of the day, they didn't really want me and Tusiime in their home. At least my brother and I were unwanted together.

Even though that was officially the end of our time with the Smiths, they did stay connected in our lives. Years later, we talked things out and came to understand each other. The Smiths continued to be supportive of us and celebrated our accomplishments. Arnie and Ilene always showed up for important events, like our high school graduations. It has been a blessing to know the Smiths. I truly thank them for warmly welcoming us into their home. Their exceptional act of kindness will never be forgotten.

15

THE RINGLEADER IN EXILE

I LIVED WITH MY TEMPORARY FAMILY FOR TWO WEEKS while the foster care program looked for a new home for me. The whole time I was there, I was very worried. I didn't know what was going on, because I only heard from the foster care program if I called them. I called every few days because I was really worried about missing school. I could only briefly find peace after I cried and prayed. I fasted, asking God to help me and just get me out of there so I could go back to school.

But soon the foster care program found a new family, and it was time for me to leave the mountains, which still felt like a different part of the world. I was so happy when they told me I was going back—I just wanted to be back in school. The morning I left, it snowed, and the person who was supposed to come get me couldn't get her car all the way up the mountain, so they decided to meet halfway. The family was sad to see me go and gave me their phone number. They hugged me so tight and told me, "Kid, you are different. Please take care of yourself and do not change. Please always call to say hi to us. We will miss you."

I got in the car of the person who was taking me to the Parkers, my new family, and waited as they talked to the family I was leaving. It always felt like the people connected with the foster care program were talking behind my back. I didn't know if what they talked about that day was good or bad, but I have always assumed it was bad. They always seemed like they were mad at me because I made their job hard. Finally, the foster program worker got in the car, and as we drove, she told me that the family really liked me. For the rest of our ride, we didn't talk much.

We pulled into a gas station where we met up with my new mom, Melinda Parker. The foster care worker put my things in the back of her black van while I introduced myself. In the car I met her baby, Enzo, and her middle child, Eddie—I tried to say hi to Eddie, but he was shy and did not say much. I love kids, and I was so pleased to think I'd get to play with them and hold them. But to be honest, what I was more excited about was that I finally was getting to go to school again and get back to my goals.

When we got to my new home, Melinda showed me my room. It was downstairs, and we had to pass through a very cold unfinished basement, but in my room, it was warm and nice.

After I had a tour of the rest of the house, I asked if I could visit where I would be going to school. She said yes, and that her oldest son, Danny, went to elementary school nearby and that we'd visit after we picked him up. The school was about ten minutes from home and looked so big. As much as I was excited to be learning again, I was sad that I could no longer attend the middle school I'd gone to when I lived with the Smiths where I'd had a good support system. I didn't know how well I'd do in this new, bigger school.

We went back home, and I started helping Danny with his

homework. Out of nowhere, he started crying, and I wondered if it might be because he had never seen a Black person before. His mom asked why he was crying, and he tried to explain. I guess he was nervous and overwhelmed. I told him that after he finished his homework, we could play together.

The dad, Chris, came home, and we all had dinner together. He was funny and warm and loved to make jokes, and he wanted to know about me and what I liked to do. After dinner, we all watched TV, and I decided to go to bed at the same time as the little kids. It had been a very long day for me.

Downstairs in my room, I felt so lonely and started crying. I hadn't seen my siblings for almost a month, although we had talked on the phone, and so I knew they were okay. I prayed and slept.

The next day, the foster care caseworker came to visit. I had only been in America six months by now, and I still did not trust the caseworkers. I could not tell if they truly cared about us. The caseworker explained that I would be going to Tibasima's house on the weekend and asked Melinda and Chris if they could drive me there and pick me up on Sunday evening. They agreed.

The houses in this neighborhood were similar to townhouses and were all built around a pond that was frozen over. It was a calm and quiet neighborhood; there weren't many kids, and I usually only saw people when the few kids that were there were waiting at the bus stop. A few church women visited the house soon after I arrived, bringing candies and cookies, but they didn't come back.

On Monday I started school. I had to wake up so early to catch the bus. I went to the bus stop and waited in the cold, listening to music through headphones. Everyone at the bus stop stared at me, the only Black girl there, and I wondered again if no one had seen a Black person before. I pretended like I did not know what was going on. Kids gave me fake smiles, but I did not smile back. I just looked at them and rolled my eyes. When the bus came, no one got on it until I got on. It was very weird. No one sat next to me, either.

The school arranged for a student to show me around the first day, which was a good thing, because the school was so crowded, it was hard to find a place to walk. You had to push through kids to get where you were going. After getting my schedule, we went to my locker, but I told the girl helping me, "I am not going to use my lock, it just gives me a headache. I will carry my bag around since the school allows us to." She took me around to all of my classes that day. While I was at that school, she was nice to me and included me, although she wasn't always nice to other kids.

My first period was biology. That class had twins who made me sit between them, which was very interesting. "There is no way I am going to be able to tell you guys apart," I told them. "You will have to bear with me." They were nice. We were lab partners, and when we were doing our assignments, they made sure I understood what I was doing. Sometimes they brought me muffins. They wanted me to hang out with them after school, but I never said yes because I needed to ask permission from a lot of people, and I would rather stay by myself. At that time, I was really closed off. I don't think I would have made a good friend then, anyway.

I didn't really get lunch at this school even though I could get it for free. The line was just too long, and the kids that I hung out with at lunch brought lunch from home. I didn't want to bring a lunch from home, as that would have been a bother for Melinda. The cafeteria was very crowded. Kids had to sit on the stairs or on the floor while eating. The kids that I hung out with always made sure to get a table—I did not know how they did it, but I was glad I had a table to sit at.

I missed going to school with Tusiime. Before, I never felt the need to make friends at school because he was always there with me. His friends sometimes ended up being my friends too. In fact, some ended up being my best friends, even today. But at this new school, there was no Tusiime, and so I had to learn how to be friendly. It was hard for me to make friends at this school because I couldn't relate to most of the kids. I did not feel like I fit in. My classmates always looked at me like I was from a different planet.

The one thing I really loved at that school was that the teachers did not treat me differently from other students. At the end of class, they asked if I needed help understanding anything. I accepted help, but I made sure I was not close with any of the teachers.

After one week of school, kids started approaching me, saying hi, and sitting in my row on the bus. I always said hi, but I didn't really interact with them much. I did not know whether I would be moving and couldn't give my best in a friendship, as trust was difficult for me then. I have been betrayed by people who I thought were friends, which hurt me. I tried to choose my friends carefully.

Three weeks after moving to the Parker home, all my remaining belongings from the Smith home were brought to me, with a wonderful surprise inside. There were postcards signed by my classmates and letters from my teachers. For an hour I read them and cried, realizing how great of a support system I had left. Some of my classmates expressed how grateful they were to meet me. I had shown them a different way to view life. They said, "You do not complain about your situation, but instead keep your head up and smile." I thought, *People like us, we cannot afford to complain.*

Sarah Smith, who made videos for us and always loved to dance with us, made a video and put it on a disk with pictures and captions. Watching it made me feel more sad and reminded me how we had hurt this family.

After a good cry, I pulled myself together. I felt like I made a mistake listening to Tibasima and wondered if I would have a future now. I realized I had hurt good people, but at the same time, I could not stay with people who I felt did not really accept me for me.

Part of me was glad we walked away and showed the foster care program we needed to live with our family. I felt like they never really listened or understood what it meant to move to a new country and get separated from the only people you know. To be fair, I hadn't realized how hard it would be, either.

Back in Uganda, when we were interviewed in preparation for going to America, the officials asked Tibasima if it was okay for us children to go into foster care and live with different people so that we could get to America sooner. When I was asked my opinion, I agreed to it, although in the end, it was a decision that my older brothers and Tibasima made that my siblings and I had to go along with.

I agreed to it mainly because I was tired of being yelled at for no reason, being blamed for everything, and taking the fall for what my siblings did. I did not really play as a child; Tibasima always wanted me home. I thought that maybe if I didn't live with her, I'd have more freedom, which I did get. But with Tibasima, I knew where I stood— when she did not like me, she showed it, but I could also tell when she appreciated something I did.

I got used to living with the Parkers, although I still did not have any real friends at school. The one thing that I loved about the Parkers was that we had honest conversations. I used to complain a lot about the foster care program to Melinda. She listened, then she told me complaining would not help anything. Until one day she told me that she did not like it when I complained about the foster care program. I didn't talk to her about it after that. It made me feel like she was on their side, and at the time, I did not want to see the situation from her point of view. The people who worked for the foster care program had become her friends.

But I believed the foster care program staff saw me as a bad kid. When they would come to the Parkers' home to see how things were going, Melinda would walk with them to the front porch as they were leaving to chat. I did not like that at all. I was sure they were talking about me, and that whatever they were saying was not good. I would grab a glass, hold it to the door, and press my ear to the glass, trying to hear what they were saying. But I never heard anything.

I have to smile when I look back on my attempts as an amateur spy, but that painful feeling of being labeled as the bad kid was no laughing matter. It seemed like the things that the foster care program was upset with my family about—us asking to live with Tibasima and our brothers and our running away from the Smiths—were all pinned on me, and me alone. I knew it was because I was the outspoken one.

I had to stop caring about what they thought of me. If I had to care about every person's opinion, I would go crazy. I stopped trying so hard for them to see me or like me. At the end of the day, I had to understand that every person would need to form their own opinion about me.

My favorite part about living with the Parkers was playing with the boys. Just holding Enzo was the best. In the spring after school, I'd go on walks with Melinda and the boys, and sometimes I gave them rides on a bike. Our favorite place was the small lake in the neighborhood, just a five-minute walk from the Parkers' house. There were fish too. Sometimes Chris and I would go fishing, but we never really caught anything.

In the summer I loved to go to the lake and sit and watch the fish, but I rarely had the time to do so. I was enrolled in a summer program for refugees sponsored by a university in a nearby city. The program was amazing and a huge help to me. It was part summer school, part support system that helped tutor and prepare us for college and under-standing how school works in America, and part fun. We had outings and did other activities, like swimming, together.

Danny didn't like that my days were tied up with the summer program. I would come back each night during the week too tired to play. And I was at Tibasima's home with my siblings on the weekends, which is when the Parkers did most of their family activities. So I did not spend as much time with the Parkers as I wished to.

I only lived with the Parkers for about three to four months, but it felt like forever. In the fall of 2015, Tibasima and my older brother finally became foster parents, and it was time for us to move back with them. They had done everything the foster care program asked them to do: They got a big apartment, a family car, finished their parenting classes, and cleared all of the other hurdles.

On my last day with the Parkers, Melinda and the kids and I were in Walmart shopping for clothes. It all suddenly hit me, and I said, "I can't believe I am leaving you guys. I guess it is for the best."

We both started crying, then Danny came to us and asked why we were both crying. We just laughed. Then on our way home, he said, "I can't believe I got two older women crying in Walmart." He for sure got his humor from his dad. Chris always joked around, saying that he is my brother because he had so many freckles they almost merged together.

Melinda drove me to my new home with my family. All her boys came with us. I was excited to move back and live with my family, to stop moving from house to house. Of course, I know that if we had not listened to Tibasima telling us to run away, we could have still been with the Smiths. I would have been in one home all that time, instead of in four homes in less than a year.

When we got to Tibasima's home, now finally my home, my siblings were already there. Everyone welcomed us and was so happy, there was only joy. As a gesture of thank you, my family had prepared food for Melinda and had juice for the kids.

It was time to say goodbye to the Parkers. It was sad, but I had to accept my journey. Even if I did not know where my path was taking me, I had to accept it. I had to understand that some people are just put in my path for short periods of time. But that also meant that I learned not to be touched by people. Whenever I made a meaningful friendship or relationship, I would move, and it hurt too much. I believed then that closing myself off during this time was the best.

I learned that some people are only briefly a part of my journey to hold me when I need safe harbor for a moment, and then to push me through to whatever comes next. I had to embrace the unknown, keep faith, keep hoping, and believe everything would all work out for the best.

16

LIVING WITH MY FAMILY

A CHANCE ENCOUNTER ON THE TRAIN made a world of difference for my family. On his commute home from work, Badulu met a kind woman named Jill. They started talking, and he told her his story. Jill was looking for a French interpreter, and since Badulu can speak French, they kept in touch. Jill and her husband, Tom, invited us to their Fourth of July party, which we really enjoyed. Tom and Jill kept checking on Tibasima and Badulu after that, helping them with rides, helping them interpret the American culture, and just overall being kind friends to us all.

Tom took us in as his own kids. Of all the men I have met in my life and who had tried to be there as a father for me, Tom was the only one who truly was successful. He listened when I complained and held me when I needed comfort. We may disagree on a lot of things, but we look far past that. Jill would pick us girls up and spend time with us while we got to know each other better. We became close. Every week, Tom and Jill would check in with us, and they treated us like family, even celebrating Christmas with us. They are still there for me today.

Jill and Tom helped Tibasima and Badulu find a bigger apartment quickly so we could move back with our family. It wasn't the safest neighborhood or the nicest apartment, but all my siblings and I cared about was that we were together. We lived as refugees in Uganda together, we came to America together, and we would stick with each other until each of us found our way.

I didn't know exactly what to expect, but I thought we would work together as a family as we did before. I did hope Tibasima would stop yelling at me.

I still didn't know if Tibasima and Badulu became our foster parents because they truly wanted us with them or because they wanted the financial support they got from the program by being our official parents. But I decided that the reason we were all together again wasn't important—if God had not wanted this to happen, it would not have happened. I accepted that my journey was meant to be this way.

Technically, I had a small sense of control over whether I would stay with my family. All I had to do was tell the foster care program that I wanted to live with a different family, and they would make that happen. Once Emma saw us back with our family, she seemed to understand finally how much our family meant to us and how being with strangers from a different culture was just too much of an adjustment. It seemed she really put herself in our shoes. And she saw we were no longer complaining to the program or the judge about our situation. And so our trust grew, and she became someone that I thought would listen to me. If I had asked her for a change, I'm sure she would have made it happen.

But I also knew I felt more comfortable and more at home with my family, and that I was tired of moving. Could I leave my family?

Yes. But would I, when I was still a kid, still exhausted, still needing support to pursue my dreams of education? No.

The first day we were all under one roof once again, we had a family meeting to decide how things were going to work in our household. The idea was supposed to be that everyone should speak up and say what they thought should change around the house. I knew this would not work. By now, Zawadi was sixteen, I was fourteen, Tusiime was thirteen, and Irini was twelve. They wanted us kids to feel like our voice was being heard, but they were not really listening. We knew that we couldn't really disagree with Tibasima, so when she talked, we just sat there quietly and listened.

I tuned everyone out for the most part, but I do remember Badulu saying, "No boyfriends. If you get boyfriends, we will not understand each other."

He was worried about us getting pregnant. African parents have a mentality that they must protect girls from men until they tell the girl she is allowed to date. I could only laugh inside at this. Parents just need to trust their girls. A woman protects herself if she doesn't want a baby. We knew it was up to us.

Besides, I was not about to start dating. I was still trying to figure myself out; to understand myself. Without knowing who I was, what could I really bring to a relationship? I only want to do something if I can give it my all and do my best.

My mind was not there. Not on dating, not even really on the family meeting. I was only thinking about how I could build myself up and make sure I was on the right path. Already, even then, I wanted to make sure that my kids would not have to go through what I went through. I didn't think to ask my siblings or Tibasima if they had any goals or what they were planning to do with their lives. I just knew

I didn't want Badulu to act like a father. I wanted him to act like a brother, to listen and be that safe space for us.

The first three months, it was all going well. We were all happy and felt like we had figured it out. It felt like we were all on the same page. But soon, things began to change.

It didn't help that we hardly spent time together. All these months, I'd dreamed of truly spending the days with my family again, like when we were together at the refugee camp. When I lived with the Smiths and Parkers, the family ate dinner together, and I hoped to do the same with my family. But we all had a different schedule. Tibasima and Alfred worked at night at a specialty meat processing plant, and they always came home smelling smoky and salty like the meat. Badulu went to community college. We barely saw him. Tusiime, Irini, and I attended the local junior high, and Zawadi was at high school. Zawadi was always the first one at home unless she stayed after school. Whenever Zawadi got home first, she would fix food for us, or sometimes Tibasima would before she left for work. The only time we had dinner or lunch together was on Sundays, and even then, sometimes someone slept through the meal because their week was too long and tiring.

We grew distant from each other, and in its own way, that prepared me for the future. I began to understand that we all have different paths in life, and one day we would not all live under one roof. Someday, our little family would grow big when we all grew up and started families of our own.

Zawadi and I were the only ones doing the housework. Tusiime's one chore was to take the trash out, and Irini did not have a chore to do unless you told her to do something. Alfred was his own person. He would cook for himself and no one else, but sometimes he made lunch for us.

That Zawadi and I were the ones who did most of the housework was so tiring because we also had homework. In particular, Zawadi had a lot because she was trying to cover ninth- and tenth-grade work all in the same school year. Zawadi never really complained. When I started complaining, I became the bad guy.

It felt like no one really cared or tried to put themselves in our shoes. Tibasima would always say, "What do you do here? You only have school, and we have school and work." At the time, Tibasima was going to school to learn English. Badulu's excuse for not doing housework was that, besides school, he was doing our foster care paperwork.

Sometimes I look back and think maybe I didn't understand my siblings and Tibasima. Maybe there was a lot going on for them. But to me, it didn't seem fair. In the other households I'd lived in—Amooti and Abwooli's home, the Smiths, the Parkers, and the family I lived with briefly—everyone did something to help with the housework. But our family expected me and Zawadi to do everything.

. . .

My new junior high was near our house, about a twenty-minute walk away. Sometimes my brothers gave us a ride to school when it snowed or when it was super cold.

At the first middle school I went to, when I lived with the Smiths, I did so well. I got all straight As in my first semester in school. I got an award for being a good student and having good grades. This motivated me to do more. This made me feel like someone saw me and my hard work.

But this new junior high school was not challenging; I felt like the teachers went easy on us. I wanted educators that pushed me beyond my comfort zone. I had the desire to learn and grow. Coming to America and starting school at the age of thirteen, I felt like I was behind. I struggled with spelling and reading properly. That feeling, like I was a meaningless girl, flared up inside me. I felt like I needed to rush things and get caught up fast to the kids my age. Otherwise, I worried I would never really feel like a human being.

At this school, it was easy to relate to people and to make friends. Most kids who went there were refugees like me. I loved the passion some kids had to change the world and help their families. I'd ask my friends what they wanted out of life and be enthralled listening to them speak with such a free spirit. But I worried I'd lose focus. At my first middle school, it was easy to focus because it was hard for me to make friends since we didn't understand each other's language.

Badulu registered my siblings and me in an after-school program specifically for refugees offered at the nearby university; we stayed in the program all through high school. It helped us a lot with our schoolwork and getting ready for college. We learned how to write essays, how to do the kind of math we needed for college, what college would be like, and how to find scholarships.

We also had sex education class with Planned Parenthood through this program. I was grateful for this class because in our communities as refugees we are not taught about sex. African parents thought that talking about sex would encourage it. Sometimes, they seemed ashamed about sex. I guess parents expected us to learn about it somehow on our own. I got an internship with Planned Parenthood and helped teach the class. It was a good experience for me and helped me advocate for my community.

Soon, it was time to think about tenth grade. Badulu's coworker Coby, who became a close family friend and like a brother to me, asked me where I was going to go to high school. I told him I did not know, but I wanted to go to a school that would challenge me to grow. He started looking into options and gave me some good suggestions, including a charter school that was an early college high school, where students earn college credits along with their high school diploma. Right after he found the school, he got us a spot just in case. After I watched videos and read about it, I knew this was the place for me. It was small and I loved the idea that I was going to get ahead.

I had to convince my brother Tusiime to go there. At first, he did not like the idea of attending a school with no sports. He wanted to go to the local high school with his friends. I had friends going there too, but I wasn't that close to them. And we had to figure out how we were going to get there, since it was in another suburb. To make it work, we needed our family on board. They would have to drop us off at the train, and after we got off the train it was still about a five-minute walk to school.

We had a family meeting about it. Badulu asked us if we were sure we wanted to go to that school. I was 10,000 percent sure, and Tusiime said he was willing to try it out. Badulu offered to take us to the train, and occasionally Alfred helped out.

That summer, my siblings and I all took two sets of summer classes from two different schools, and were in class from 8 a.m. to 5 p.m. Our motivation was to help Zawadi—by doing a double load of summer classes, she would be able to graduate on time. It was our way of saying, "Sis, we are behind you." Zawadi and I did a lot of reading that summer, about six books each. To me, those were fun times. But I was ready to start my new journey at my new high school.

17

COFFEE AND CHEMISTRY

I REALLY LOVED THE EARLY COLLEGE HIGH SCHOOL because it was a small school and I was able to get ahead. But it was challenging for me—I still struggled to read English properly, and I did not know how to write an essay. But I was still expected to do the same work as everyone else, and I loved that challenge.

Before school started, we had a whole week of orientation. It was so intimidating, but I was so excited and ready to grow. That week showed me I made the right choice, even though I did not know how I was going to do it all. Tusiime did not say anything about how he felt. He always seemed happy. He made new friends easily, and once again girls were all over him. Orientation week I only made one friend, but that was enough for me at that moment.

The first week of school was living Hell. I am not a huge fan of math, and our teacher did not really explain the problems. Her way of teaching did not make sense to me. I thought I was the only one, but other students were saying the same thing. My English class assigned homework requiring us to write about ourselves. I hated talking about myself. I was not even sure where to begin.

My history class was easy. The teacher lectured well, and he challenged our ways of thinking. Even when we wanted to go deep into history, you could tell that there were things he was not allowed to talk about. And so after class, I always did my own reading. I wanted to know why so many people think America is the greatest country when it has its own problems. I wanted to understand why America and its systems were the way they were.

I had hours of homework to do every night. I'd do my math homework with friends at school, then ride the train home, cook, eat, take a shower, and sit and do my homework until 2 a.m. or sometimes even 3 a.m. I would wake up at 6 a.m. to get to school on time. Coffee became my best friend.

My older brothers always warned me about drinking too much coffee each morning, when I'd make us stop at the gas station for coffee on our way to the train. But it was the only way I knew how to stay awake. I had to drink a lot of water too. Saturdays were my one day to sleep in, but it wasn't a completely free day—I had church choir practice in the afternoons. On Sundays after church, I made sure I slept. This was my life my sophomore year.

I worried I wasn't sleeping enough, and sometimes I thought maybe I made a bad choice to go to early college high school. But I was willing to take risks and do what it took to learn and grow. I became independent in everything except my finances, for which I was still dependent on the foster care program. I told myself that not getting enough sleep and drinking so much coffee every morning was just temporary; I'd get the hang of the workload.

In September we started back up with attending the refugee afterschool program. After school I would ride the train all the way to the university and then walk to the program building, but I would get a ride back home. This program played a big part in my high school success—if it weren't for the support of their tutors on my math and essays, I would have failed my math and English classes.

I took chemistry my sophomore year. Chemistry was hard and challenging, but I loved how it made me think in a different way. It was another way to look at faith, to believe that things happen even if we don't have the ability to see them. And the lab work taught me patience (something I didn't have a lot of then).

But I struggled with tests in chemistry class, and so one day I went to my chemistry teacher and said, "I may be the only one doing bad in your class."

She told me I wasn't.

"How can I improve?" I asked.

"Well, you read the textbooks, and you do well on our quizzes. Your presentations and projects are well done and creative. You even do better than the kids who speak English as their first language. I am very impressed," she said. "It is only the tests you score low on, even though I see you studying with your friends."

She walked me through the test. I was nervous. She would ask me a question that I failed on the test, and I would get it right. She told me to keep doing what I was doing. "We will work something out," she told me.

As I walked outside of the classroom, she told me, "Do not worry, you are one of my best students. You are in the top of your class. The one thing about you is that you do not make excuses about your situation, even though you could make a lot. You just go for it. I am proud of you."

That was nice to hear from a teacher, but I was not about to let it go to my head. I never wanted to give myself credit for doing things.

I just moved on to what I needed to do next, motivated by both my past and my future. I would tell myself, I am going to get an education because I was not given the chance at an earlier age to prepare a better future for the next generation of my family.

Through my high school classes, I got an opportunity to take a chemistry class at the university in the summer of my sophomore year. My teacher told the class about the course and that it was eight college credits. If we were interested, she would nominate us and we would get a partial scholarship. I hoped the foster care program would help me pay for the rest, so I asked my teacher to nominate me because I wanted to take the class. I went home and asked Badulu to ask the foster care program if they could pay for it, but they said their policy was they would pay for high school tutoring, but not for a college class. I was so disappointed.

Frankly, I was more than disappointed, I was frustrated. The foster care program often had us come to large dinners and celebrations they hosted to showcase their program to donors and government groups. They singled us out as the best kids in the program in terms of our passion for our education and grades. To hold us out as a success story in public but not help us more behind the scenes felt hypocritical to me. We'd asked for financial support for laptops, and that had been refused. But even small requests for items related to school we had to negotiate. Refusing to help me with the chemistry class was just one more let down in a succession of disappointments.

A week later, I got an email saying that I had to pay the rest of the money to secure my spot in class. I forwarded the email to Badulu, telling him how much I wanted this opportunity and asking if he knew anyone who could step in and help. I replied to the chemistry course program, asking that they please give me a few days to find the funds. They agreed and gave me a new deadline. But when I went to the course orientation, I found out that my spot was given away. I spoke to them and explained my situation, and they let me sit through the orientation.

I listened to everything they had to say, but inside I was full of disappointment because I knew I was not going to get to take this class. I felt like I had failed myself, and I cried all the way home on the train. When Badulu picked me up from the train station, I sat in the back of the car. I did not want him to see my face. He asked me how it went.

"They gave my spot away," I said sadly. "But they said if anyone drops out, they will let me know."

"I am sorry, it was a great opportunity for you," he said.

"You really do not know anyone who can pay that amount?" I asked.

"No," he said. "But I will reach out to the refugee scholarship fund and pray that someone drops out."

Soon, I received an email saying that someone had dropped out of class and that I could have the place and the scholarship and that I should find a research position to pay for the rest of the fees. Badulu found out that the refugee scholarship fund was willing to sponsor me. I was overjoyed! I gave him a big hug and told him how much I appreciated him.

The research position was through the SEED Project (Seeking Educational Equity and Diversity). At first I did not know how I was going to do the research on top of an eight-credit class, but luckily they were flexible about when I conducted my research hours.

I took a moment to think about how many people it took for me just to take this class. That moment made me realize how blessed I was. I was so grateful in my heart. I now understood that when a child is in a mother's womb, that child is only for that one person. But once they are born, they belong to us all. And the people that see that and support all children are a gift to our world.

I ended my sophomore year stronger than ever. I had grown so much—I'd taken on academic challenges while improving skills like reading English well and writing essays that American children had the support to master at a much younger age. And I'd secured ways to get ahead in my education. I had started writing this book the year before, and now I worked on improving it.

. . .

By this time I knew more people, and I had created a small group of friends. I became close at school with two girls who were cousins, and I learned about a different kind of chemistry, the kind between friends that can be just as volatile.

One cousin, Murungi, I was very close to, and the other, Omusuma, never really accepted me. She always treated me wrong. I decided that was her problem, not mine. I treated Omusuma right, and I accepted her. I gave her a chance and celebrated her accomplishments, but I never really got the same energy from her. I always tried to include her in things, but she was so negative toward life and mean for no reason. I did not understand if she was just mean to me or to everyone.

We got into fights sometimes. I hated the way Omusuma treated her cousin—sometimes she was so mean she made Murungi cry. I could see Murungi did not really know how to defend herself. It was not really my place, but I always asked Murungi why she let Omusuma treat her that way.

One day, I texted Omusuma and asked, "Do you not like me because I am Black?" At that time, I was the only Black person and the only refugee in the school. I didn't experience overt racism, but I did always stand out as different.

She texted back, "No."

"Why do you treat me the way you do?" I asked. No answer. When I saw her in person I asked again. Still she said nothing.

I was not about to let her negative feelings get to me. I was still struggling with my childhood trauma of being told I was meaningless. From then on, I tried to ignore her.

One day at school after lunch, we all went to the bathroom. Murungi always wore rings and would take them off to wash her hands. I started playing around with her, and I told her I flushed them. Of course I didn't, and she knew I was joking. Omusuma stepped in and said so many rude things to me. She grabbed my wallet out of my bag and said she was going to flush my credit cards down the toilet.

I told her to go ahead.

I gave Murungi her rings back, left the bathroom, and went to class. I was hurt that Omusuma would take a silly moment and turn it mean, but at the same time, I was surprised that I felt calm afterward. Omusuma was lucky she knew the new Desange. If she had tried that on the old Desange, I would have fought her for disrespecting me like that.

Murungi followed me and apologized on Omusuma's behalf. I told Murungi that she did not have to apologize to me. People need to take responsibility for their own actions.

"I don't think I want to be around her anymore," I said. "I cannot even be her friend. You and I can always talk."

That evening on my way home on the train, I texted Omusuma. I told her that I truly saw her; I saw that she was in a lot of pain. But I also told her how negative she was and to stop being mean to her cousin, because she was the only person who had been there for her. I told her I had tried to be a friend and a sister. I said, "I gave you a chance, but you were too blind to see it." I said my piece. Then I deleted her number and blocked her everywhere she could contact me.

The sad part for me was I knew my relationship with Murungi was going to wind down anyway—the semester was ending, and she was not coming back to my high school the next year.

The next day I had to try to find new friends. This time making new friends was not as hard, and these new friendships developed into long-term connections. I always said hi to Murungi when we crossed paths, and sometimes we went to McDonald's together. Omusuma tried to say hi to me, but I would simply shake my head no. I could tell she was trying to be friends with me, but I was done. And I wasn't about to look back.

At the end of the school year, when everyone was signing year-books, Omusuma asked if she could sign mine. I allowed it, and she wrote an apology and said she hoped we could be friends again. I could tell her apology was sincere. I felt her pouring her heart out. In my heart, I had forgiven her a long time ago; I always thought she was just figuring herself out and didn't know how to deal with people or how to be in a friendship. But I did not understand why she wanted to be friends with me again when she was the one who pushed me away. Life moves on and I was ready to start my summer at the university.

I wasn't the only one ready to move on. Zawadi graduated high school (in only two and a half years) and got a full scholarship to the same university. She decided to start right away that summer. I was so proud of her and all her success. But I was also worried about Zawadi leaving home and us not living together. I knew once Zawadi was gone, it would be me doing the cleaning and cooking by myself. I would be the only one Tibasima would yell at whenever she was angry about something. I still had so much schoolwork to do, and what little free time I had was about to get even smaller.

Zawadi had always been there. She was someone I talked to and who listened to all my crazy stories and put up with me when I was tough to deal with. She had been to Hell and back with me. She was not just my sister but also my best friend, and the only person I was close to in the family.

She told me not to worry and that she would always come back home for the weekends. But I knew it was not going to be the same. I knew I was going to be lonely without her home. I knew that at some point we would take different paths, and it was not yet my time to leave home yet. I just had to trust God that I would be okay at home without her.

18

MY JOURNEY TO
UNIVERSITY BEGINS

ON MY FIRST DAY OF THE SUMMER CHEMISTRY CLASS, I saw all these kids from different schools—only a handful of the students came from my high school. I was excited, but when the professor started teaching and told us that the class would be fast-paced, I worried about how I would manage. *Here we go,* I thought. *Lord, take the wheel. I know you have allowed me to be in this class, but I am not sure how I am going to survive. Help me to find the strength to learn all I can.*

The first day of the class felt like we'd jumped into the middle of a semester. The professor reviewed the basic chemistry I'd already learned. It felt like he covered all of high school chemistry in three days. The professor was very personable. When I went to his office hours, we talked like we had known each other for a long time. After answering all my questions about class, he would ask me about my life and point of view and then share his.

We would have class in the morning, then we would have labs after class before lunch. We were assigned to small groups that made it easy to make friends.

A week after class was in session, I started working in the research lab. The first day, I shadowed a PhD student who explained to me what I would be doing, but English wasn't his first language either, so I was a little lost. I was going to research resistive pulse sensing of nanoparticles. I had no idea what that was. It turned out that my job was to measure nanoparticles by recording how much current they displaced. Once the PhD student demonstrated it to me, I understood. The work had to be repeated multiple times as part of the research, and some days, the work would not go as planned, and I would not get anything done.

One day I asked the PhD student if he always had to repeat himself so much with the research he did.

"Yes," he laughed. "You have to be so patient."

I was the most impatient person you would meet. I hate repeating myself, but with this research, I had to. I learned so much—as a student but also as a person—but most of all, I learned about patience.

Trying to manage the work for my class lab and my research lab at the same time was interesting. I barely had free time that summer. Most days I got home at 6 p.m., ate, then went straight to bed because I was very tired. My days were long, but I was proud of myself for what I was doing.

However, I felt so lonely at home during the week, when Zawadi was on campus. The house was too empty. I barely saw Tusiime and Irini. I mostly only saw my family on the weekends. Some days I saw Zawadi on campus, and we would grab lunch together. I never told her how I felt about her leaving home. In my head, it was my battle to learn how to live without her.

I had to pretend everything was fine, but I was getting sick. Lack of sleep, eating infrequently and a lot of junk food, and all of the stress and worry triggered a flare up of my ulcers. Zawadi called every morning to make sure I ate or at least drank milk, because milk does help a lot.

The summer was coming to an end. It had been an honor to work with the research lab, and I really enjoyed both the research lab and chemistry class. I didn't do as well in the class as I had hoped to, but I did pass. And two weeks later, the final years of my high school journey began.

. . .

My junior year was not as bad as my sophomore year. I got more sleep and drank less coffee. It did not take me that long to write my essays, and I could read English well.

Zawadi came home more, almost every weekend, and we talked about how college life works. I could tell how stressed she was. She said I was lucky my high school was preparing me for college. It always felt nice to have her home.

In the middle of my junior year, Tusiime decided to change schools. He was not doing well at the early college high school. As much as I wanted him to stay, I had to support him in his decision. But it was hard for me—Tusiime and I had always gone to school together, and without him, I was so lonely during my school day and especially during my long train commute.

Now that we were all at different schools, we had to help each other be on time. Tusiime often woke me up before he had to leave for the school bus, and I would wake up Irini before I left for the train so that she wouldn't miss the city bus she took to her school. I was happy each of us had found the right school for us, but since we were not spending enough time together, we started growing apart. Tusiime and I in particular barely saw each other, and I felt sad that we were not as close as we used to be. I tried to work hard and rebuild our connection, but with new friends, he had little time for his sister. I did not want to force it, so I just let it be.

During my junior year, I took more college classes, which took up most of my time. I also started tutoring kids in our apartment complex who were new refugees. I helped them read and write English and helped with their homework. Because of this, I cut back my hours at the after-school program. I loved the drive these kids had to succeed and how much they wanted to learn and know how things worked.

I started applying for scholarships for university with the help of the after-school refugee program. They would help us figure out which scholarships to apply to and review our application essays.

Members of my church suggested I enter the Miss Juneteenth competition, which brings awareness about the Juneteenth holiday that commemorates the day, two years after the US Civil War ended, when enslaved Blacks in Galveston, Texas, finally learned they'd been emancipated. All that was required was to submit an essay. I was honored and pleased to win, which earned me a small scholarship for school.

I also continued work on writing through a teen writing program our family friend, Coby, paid for me to attend. In this program, they gave you a mentor who you met with every Saturday or during the week to work on writing. I used this opportunity to work on my personal statements that I'd use for college applications.

I had always wanted to become a doctor. During my junior year, I took a step toward that dream by getting certified as a nurse assistant

(CNA). A good friend and I took the classes we needed to earn the certification from 6 p.m. to 10 p.m. She had a car and would give me a ride to class. After class she would drive me to the train station and wait with me until the train got there since it was already dark and so cold. The city buses didn't run that late, so I had to walk home from the train station in the dark if Badulu couldn't pick me up. I carried scissors in my pocket for those walks home, just in case, scary scenarios running through my mind: What if someone shoots me? Or kidnaps me? I'd imagine the worst scenarios as I walked home on the dark streets, then come up with a plan of what I would do if they happened.

After I got my certification, I worked as a CNA for a month before it got to be too much. Seeing people at their worst and so hopeless was hard for me. I worked with a young man who got shot in the back and would never walk again. He was so mad all the time. We would always talk about what a surprise life can be. He shared his story with me as I made his bed—all I could do was cry. That day I realized how blessed I was. He asked me, "If you were in my situation what would you do?"

I told him I would accept my situation and embrace it because it was something that I would not have control over. But I told him that it would probably take me a long time to accept it. I would keep trying to learn how to walk and keep hoping, believing, praying, and fasting.

He said, "How do you even accept something like this?"

I told him the short version of my life story and the trauma I'd been through and said, "I accepted it and did what I could about what was within my control. Then I let God take the wheel. I kept hoping and believing and having faith that one day life would change for me, too. There was no point of feeling sorry for myself about things I couldn't change. Being negative would just make me suffer more. I refused to be a victim. I chose to be a warrior."

I choose to see the world as a positive place. I choose to see good in people even when others see the worst in them. Some CNAs are so mean to their patients. I always put myself in people's shoes to try to understand them.

I didn't like the CNA work environment. Some CNAs just had a negative attitude. I didn't like how they treated patients. Also, dealing with blood and other things most people get squeamish about was not a big deal to me, but I found it hard to have the patience that was needed for this work. I started rethinking my decision to go to medical school. I thought maybe I could go into healthcare and just cut myself off emotionally and try not to care. But then, the work wouldn't be meaningful to me, and that wasn't what I wanted.

My junior year of high school—a great year for me—came to an end. I returned to the chemistry program that summer and also took online college courses during the day and classes at the local community college at night. It was time to get ready for my final year of high school and take the last steps toward my dream of a university education.

19

FINDING MY OWN WAY

THE SUMMER BEFORE MY SENIOR YEAR OF HIGH SCHOOL, my family moved to a new neighborhood I liked, but it was going to be a long journey to get to school for me and Irini, who was going to join me at the early college high school. We had lots of ways to get there, but every option involved a combination of buses or trains or both and walking. Tusiime had to walk twenty minutes to get on a city bus, which took him to the school bus. With our crazy travel, we barely saw each other. We barely talked or did fun things together anymore. We were no longer close; it felt like everyone in our family was on their own journey. I did not like the way things were going, but I accepted it. Outside of the house, we still put on the face that we were close.

I was so excited to start my final year of high school. I would be graduating with an associate of applied science degree and a high school diploma and felt well prepared for university.

I did not have a lot of classes to take, but I still went early in the morning to school with Irini. My little sister is not a morning person. She would not say even a single word in the morning. I would try to make conversation with her on the train and bus, but she wouldn't say anything. So I stopped going early, and I slept in instead. Of course, I was still her alarm clock every morning, waking her up so she was not late.

While my class load was smaller, I was still very busy. I applied to schools, went to interviews, and applied for scholarships to add to the ones I'd already secured during my junior year. I also took part in FutureINDesign, which gives students like me the opportunity to improve our technology skills, work with professionals on real projects, and earn school credit. I learned how to code, which I never completely mastered, although I was good at the designing part. I was glad I had this experience to learn that IT is not my thing at all. It's important to know not just what you can do, but what is a good fit for you.

I wanted a part-time job and needed something that fit my crazy schedule. So I took a position as a janitor at my school, which meant most of the time I was the last person in the school building. There were days when I cleaned the bathrooms and there were days I vacuumed the whole school. This job really opened my eyes and made me appreciate the people who clean public buildings. It wasn't just good work, it was also a chance to find out who my true friends were. Two friends really helped with that job—one was also a janitor and would trade shifts with me when I needed it. We became close, and she helped me whenever I was going through hard times. And one day, two boys walked up to me and said they wanted to help me clean. I was very surprised, and they made my day when they asked to help me.

That year I was very worried about getting enough scholarship money. Without it, there would be no education for me. I felt so tired and drained. I did not feel like doing anything, so it was a good thing I had help writing essays and personal statements for my applications the year before. It got so hard to wake up in the morning and to get out of bed. I rode Uber to school a lot—that took up a lot of my personal allowance I got from the foster care program, but it was worth it. But most of the time Tom took us to school. Without Tom I don't know how I could have survived.

I took a chance on a fun opportunity that really paid off. Friends of mine had participated in the Miss Africa Utah pageant, and I'd gone to support them and thought it seemed fun. Plus, if I won, I'd get a scholarship, so I decided to try.

The pageant also gave me another new experience—putting makeup on my face for the first time! I didn't know a thing about makeup and none of my friends could help me. Luckily, a makeup artist named Akiiki, who had just moved to Utah, reached out on Instagram to all the girls who were running for Miss Africa Utah that year and offered a free trial to see if we wanted to use her services.

But getting to Akiiki's home to have my makeup done was its own issue. Tom was teaching me to drive, and I was working hard to earn my license to be eligible for the funds the foster care program had promised us we could use to purchase a car. The program said we could have $1,000 each. Tusiime and I planned to pool our money to buy a car to share, but they said we had to have our driver's licenses first.

Once I earned my license, I asked the program for the money, but they said no. They said that money was a reward for good behavior; I didn't deserve the money to put toward a car because I had been a bad kid. I couldn't believe it! They'd never said that the car money was a reward. And they wouldn't even tell me specifically what I'd done not to deserve it. Yet again, the foster care program lost my trust.

So now I had to rely on the kindness of friends like Tom and even my caseworker to get me to Akiiki. Sometimes, since I was dependent on them and their schedules, I had to arrive early, but that was fun, too, because I got to play with Akiiki's little boy.

When Akiiki did my makeup as a test for the first time, I really loved it, and booked her for the pageant events right away. Thankfully, Badulu was kind enough to pay for her services. After the pageant, I kept modeling for Akiiki, and she became a friend, sister, mentor, and family member. I learned so much from her about the entertainment industry. She also helped Irini start her modeling career. And she helped me with ideas as I created unDEfeated.

The pageant was a great experience in so many ways. I had the opportunity to represent my country and to be able to serve as Miss Democratic Republic of Congo Utah 2019. And I won a small scholarship to a program that taught problem-solving skills. My platform during the pageant was to educate youth about refugees, since I felt like people did not really understand much about us. The director of an organization that works with refugees in Utah helped create those education opportunities after the pageant. I also created a club at my school where I could talk with kids about refugees, and as a club, we volunteered with the refugee center on Saturdays. I met a lot of great people, some of whom are my mentors today.

All along I kept working on getting into and paying for university. My hopes were on getting accepted to the University of Utah with a full scholarship from the David Eccles School of Business First Ascent Scholars Program.

That application process was not easy. I had multiple interviews, some of which felt very personal. They asked me to talk about things that I did not even talk about with my siblings. There is nothing I hated more than being vulnerable with people. For that interview, I had to be vulnerable with people that I didn't even know and that I had never met in my life. I was sure that these people were not going to like me after I was vulnerable with them. After one interview, I went to the bathroom and cried so hard, releasing so much emotion I had been holding inside for so long.

Other friends had heard they'd been accepted, but I hadn't. Then, I got an email asking me to go to the First Ascent office. I rode the train and walked through pouring rain to learn my fate. The program staff was so happy to see me and gave me the news that I had gotten the scholarship, but they couldn't send out the letter because I had not been accepted to the University of Utah yet.

They asked how the process was going, and I explained that I took a college class at the local community college that also served as credit for my high school English class, but that the university did not accept it. So, I was finishing up a class for that high school English credit online with the help of the after-school refugee program. They said they'd hold my spot for the scholarship and work with me to figure out everything. They said that everyone who interviewed me loved me, and how grateful they were to have me in the program.

Riding the train back to school that day, my mind was so calm. I could not believe that I was going to go to university and continue my education alongside my sister, Zawadi. On the train, as I looked out the window at the snow, I thought back on my journey. I came here not knowing how to read and write English. All my siblings and I lived a life we never saw coming. My heart that day was filled with gratitude.

So many people celebrated with me. My friend from the CNA work hugged me and jumped up and down like she was the one that got the scholarship. I texted Zawadi, and she sent me a voice recording, yelling, "Congratulations girl!" But I took my time telling the rest of my family. After about two weeks, I shared the news with Alfred,

Tusiime, and Irini, but not Tibasima or Badulu. I did not know what Tibasima's reaction would be and didn't want to spoil my happiness.

I graduated from the early college high school on May 15, 2019. I was so incredibly happy. I could not believe that I graduated, especially after being told that I would not even get my high school diploma, that I would not achieve anything with my life, that I was a meaningless girl. At that moment, while riding in an Uber to my graduation I thought: *Fight the good fight of life with all your might and face your problems with courage, commitment, and perseverance. Just keep moving forward with optimism in your heart, and your success will come. No one but you and God can determine your journey.*

20

CUT THE TIES THAT BIND

THE WEEK OF MY GRADUATION, I told Badulu and Tibasima that I got a full scholarship to the University of Utah. Badulu told me congratulations and that he was proud of me. At first, Tibasima smiled. But then, I told her how soon I'd be leaving in order to participate in the summer programs that went along with my scholarship. Tibasima wanted me to wait until the fall semester started because she had a new baby and wanted help. But Zawadi was home for the summer and Irini would still be home and both could help. She didn't really need me, and I was unhappy at home and ready to leave.

And she may have had other reasons to want me to stay beyond the baby. I told her and Badulu that I no longer needed to be in the foster care program. Tibasima disagreed—she did not want the financial support to be taken away when I left. Badulu told me he would talk with the program about my leaving, but he never did. That made me think he also wanted the financial support to keep coming.

I left home in June. The entire family knew that once I was out the door, I would not look back.

My whole family took me to my dorm to officially start my university journey. I said goodbye to Tibasima in the kitchen, and she cried, which surprised me—I was expecting one of her usual lectures. I told her not to cry.

After my family left, I went on a hike by myself. I cried so much on that hike. I felt so lonely, but at the same time, I felt like I just got out of prison. I felt like a weight had been lifted off my shoulders. Tibasima's tears had moved me, but I knew that she had to know this day had been a long time coming. She always thought the worst of me and treated me in a way that did not give me peace—surely she'd known that once I could leave, I would.

There were days when I felt like going back to spend a night with my family, but there in that household, something always held me back, and I just didn't want to be in that environment again. Tibasima and Badulu held on to the old ways—I had to ask permission to do anything (and the answer was often no). Too often I felt they didn't see my potential—they worried about boyfriends, believing I'd get pregnant and have to get married or live on the streets, when what was on my mind wasn't boys, it was education. I wanted to find myself and know what I was capable of. It was time for me to take this journey without my family.

. . .

I did not take a break. A mere week after high school graduation, I was already hard at work in my university summer programs. I did the refugee summer program again, and added the QuestBridge and First Ascent summer programs, both of which helped us learn about college work, culture, and resources we could turn to. Doing all three at once was hard, but I enjoyed it all. In addition to university preparation classes, the First Ascent program offered fun activities and put us in cohorts so that we could build friendships and start our first year at the university with peers that we could lean on for support.

As my new world began to take shape, I realized there was one more tie to my old world that I needed to sever. I was eligible to stay in the foster care program until I was twenty-one, but it was time for me to end that relationship. My frustration and distrust had been building for many years, but two things happened that signaled it was time for me to walk away. First, our caseworker, Emma, was fired. It had taken years, but I'd grown to trust Emma, and only Emma. And then suddenly, she was gone, and a man I didn't know had taken her place.

The second thing was that the foster program assumed they had the right to access my university grades and financial aid information, and insisted I give them my login information and passwords for my accounts in the university system. I did not see how they could feel justified invading my privacy in that way. They'd never asked for this information in high school, neither I nor my family had been told before this point, as far as I knew, that we were required to give them this information. Especially since the foster care program did not pay for my tuition, I didn't see how they had the right to access my accounts. I truly felt disrespected by the foster care program.

It was time to take matters into my own hands. And rather than petition the court to leave the foster care program, which could have been an ugly process, I decided to take the clean way out: I began my application for US citizenship. Since I was eighteen, once I became a US citizen, I would automatically exit the program. I filled out the application right away, then studied online for the citizenship test throughout my freshman year.

The summer of my first year, I shared a dorm room with another student, and we got along well. I also kept up with Akiiki, my sister Zawadi, who was a junior at the university, and another friend. But I really didn't share much with them, and definitely closed myself off from people outside of that small circle. I didn't really try to make any new friends. At home, I stayed in my bedroom, even if people I knew were visiting my roommate. I didn't really want to be a part of activities. I did not really go out. Whenever I was asked on a date, I turned it down. Whenever my friends asked me to go out, I would usually say no. The few times I would try to go, I didn't feel present. I stopped singing in church. All I did was go to class, work, and go back to my room, and I started to gain weight. I missed having a family around me, even though I didn't want to be back with Tibasima.

I took on a part-time job that I went to in the evenings. When winter came and it got dark early, it would already be dark when work ended. I never saw the sun. Homework kept me busy after work, but at the same time I felt like something was missing. I felt like I was not doing anything with my life.

I went into a depression. I was fighting inside myself every day, and beat myself up, feeling like I was not accomplished. Whenever I felt it was too much, I would go to Zawadi's dorm to sleep over without explaining what was bothering me. Zawadi always noticed that I was not myself, but she never asked why. She knows not to push me, that over time I will open up to her.

I thought maybe I should go to see a therapist, but I was not ready to open up to anyone. I hated talking about my emotions. So I tried to imagine that I was happy. I pushed myself to see all the blessings that I'd been given, to look back and see how far I'd come. I was proud, but at the same time, I did not have a sense of fulfillment. I felt like I was stupid and like what I was doing was not good enough. I even lost my faith at that time. My world was falling apart even when everything seemed to be good. I felt like I was fighting a battle that I couldn't win. I did not know what was going on with me.

But on the outside, everyone saw me as good, as a success. I continued to work with the director of the refugee nonprofit to educate youth about refugees. I gave a lot of speeches to middle schools and high schools throughout Utah, and the kids seemed to be inspired.

Only once did I reluctantly accept my friends' urgings to join them out at a party. Understand it's not all parties that disinterest me. When it comes to parties, it is not about food or people for me, it is all about the music and dancing. I love African or Latino parties because the music is so good, but the music at American parties was not for me.

But this one time, I decided to give it a try. When we got there, everyone was so surprised that I showed up. It was a crowded house party—definitely not my thing—and of course there was plenty of drinking and smoking and who knows what else going on. My friend gave us a ride, and said to me when dropping us off, "If you want to leave just call me, and I will come get you."

I didn't really have fun at this party. It wasn't my scene; I just didn't get this kind of fun. And thirty minutes after we got there, it turned not fun real quick. The police came. I started freaking out. Not only were my friends and I not twenty-one yet, but if I were arrested for being underage at a party with alcohol, even if I didn't drink, I knew it would affect my citizenship application. I knew I could pass as twenty-one because of my appearance; people always told me that I looked older than I was. I was praying that this would play in my favor.

The police stood in the door, checking IDs before they let people pass through. My friends and I hid in the laundry room and called our friend to come get us. There was a girl there who was trying to hide in the washing machine. It was obvious how drunk she was—besides her ridiculous attempt to hide, she was slurring her words—so we kicked her out of the room. Other people were jumping out of the laundry room window, hoping to elude the police, but they surrounded the house, so there really was no escape.

We stayed in the laundry room hoping the police would not destroy the whole house as they searched for partiers. Eventually, they found us. But they did not even ask for our IDs, they just let us go.

My friends looked for another party, but I told them to drop me off at home and go on without me. We did have a good laugh about how I finally went to my first college party and the police showed up. I decided it wasn't just my first party, it was my last. If I was going to get in trouble, I wanted to at least have fun doing it.

Instead of parties, I spent my free time trying to fill that hole in me, trying to find that sense of fulfillment that was eluding me. My part-time job was with Utah Community Action, a nonprofit dedicated to fighting poverty. I really enjoyed the opportunity to work with under-served communities. Seeing what other people were going through was eye-opening. It made me appreciate what I had and all the people that supported me and pushed me to be the woman I am today. And that gave me an idea of what I wanted to do in my career—to be that support for other women like me somehow.

I also got to take a trip with a business scholars program to San Francisco, California. It was only the second time I'd been outside of Utah since arriving in America. I loved seeing a new city, which surprisingly reminded me a little of home, thanks to the sounds and smells of the ocean and the palm trees everywhere. That trip sparked a love of travel in me. Finishing the work to earn my US citizenship would make traveling possible.

Before my first year of university ended, the COVID-19 pandemic hit. We finished our courses online, and I got laid off from my job. It felt like everything went crazy. As the number of COVID cases got worse and so many people died, it felt like the world was falling apart. I thought, *Here we go, the end of the world is here, just like the Book of Revelation said*. I did not know what else to think about what was happening in the world, and I worried that all of my negative feelings about myself must be true.

It took me a while to accept the concept of online work and life, but I did learn to accept it and navigate it successfully, and I was grateful only those last couple of weeks of my first year were impacted.

On my last day of classes, I took a moment to reflect. I didn't really do as well in my classes as I would have liked to. Mostly because I did not have the same drive I'd always had. I accomplished a lot that year, but at the time I did not recognize that. I'm very hard on myself, and rarely give myself credit and find it difficult to receive praise from others.

The summer of 2020, I took my test and became a US citizen, which meant I also got a passport. Now, I could travel and study abroad in the future.

But for that summer I stayed on campus, taking classes and working with the University of Utah to help people to get tested for COVID. It was a good job, and I was on my feet all day, and it was good for my health to get that exercise at work. Other changes helped my health improve: I cooked healthy dinners for myself and slept very well. I had time to do more modeling, which I enjoyed. Toward the end of the summer, I changed jobs to working with the local health department to call people about their COVID test results. That was a work-from-home position, which I knew would work better for my fall class schedule. I kept up my exercise with hikes either by myself or sometimes with Zawadi, who was living close by. Alfred visited often, and I saw friends through work, too.

But possibly the best change in terms of my emotional health was that, because of COVID, I had a whole dorm room to myself that summer. I learned that I love being by myself, and I used solitude to start discovering myself, beginning with meeting myself where I was.

I allowed myself to be vulnerable. For once in my life, I accepted I am a human being and put my ego aside. I decided it was okay to feel all the weird emotions. It's okay to feel lost sometimes.

I had always been scared of being emotional. I always pushed my emotions away. I was taught growing up that showing emotions made me weak, and that I had to show the world I was strong. For the longest time in my life, I was disconnected from my feelings. Except for the worst moments of my life, I rarely cried. Tibasima would beat me up, and I still would not cry.

Growing up I did not have a soft place inside of me. Looking back, I think that is why I was so mean. I never really put myself in the shoes of the kids that I bullied. But now, I allowed myself to relive all the painful moments of my past and understand why I did things the way I did them. Going through dark times really helped me to find myself again. I allowed myself to go through whatever I was going through. I did not push my emotions away. It allowed me to be a human being and see how emotions help me relate to other people, to understand what they are going through. I still find emotions hard, but now I know they do not make me weak, they make me strong. And knowing the power of emotions, I started, and now continue, to try to surround myself with as much positivity as possible.

I was able to pinpoint something I wanted that I didn't have—I wanted to feel fulfilled. I still continued educating companies and groups—over Zoom instead of in person—about being a refugee and started to branch out as an inspirational speaker. And then I heard from friends in Uganda who needed help. Since I had a full scholarship that covered my expenses, I already used the wages from my jobs to help people in Uganda. I sponsored three students with school tuition and sent money to my Ugandan families for food and hospital expenses. But so many people reached out to me, and I wanted to find a way to help more.

Every night after work and my online classes, I would research how to work with underserved communities, which gave me the idea to start a nonprofit organization. When I looked into it more, I could see it was a lot of work, and thought this was not for me. I started talking myself out of the idea. Then one night I was sitting on my couch going through my old photos, and I came across a photo of my family and I at the airport in Uganda the day we left for America. I looked at those photos and thought, *Someone fought for me to have the life I have today*. This nonprofit is not about me and what I find hard to do. It is about giving back to communities. I thought about all the people who have supported me and my full scholarship to university. I knew it was time.

But I didn't rush it. I started slowly and thoughtfully, doing more of my own research. I knew that starting a nonprofit would be a work in progress for quite a while, but I also knew I had to take this path.

21

FINDING MY VOICE

MY SECOND YEAR OF COLLEGE, COVID was still causing everything to be online. In the winter, this turned into a blessing for me. I am not a fan of cold, and it was nice to not have to get up early and bundle up to get to class through a bitter, chilling wind. Soon the temptation to just wake up, roll over, and log in to class became too great (especially when I sometimes fell back asleep during a class). So I came up with a new plan: I would wake up and get dressed up as if I was going to class in person, then I would go somewhere that felt like class so I could focus and actually learn something.

With staying focused in class sorted out, I now needed to figure out how to start my nonprofit when the world still met each other online. I was used to meeting up with people and expressing in person how I needed the help from them. But in January of 2021, I got a fortuitous message. NextGen, a company that mentors entrepreneurs, invited me to talk at an event. I learned about their organization and was intrigued, and even though I ended up not speaking, I attended the event and met a lot of interesting people who were interested in learning more about my ideas for a nonprofit, some who eventually became mentors. As I talked about what I envisioned for my nonprofit, it evolved from an idea to a plan taking shape.

I started to move quickly after that, getting help from various people with the legal formation of my organization and identifying board members. I kept working on my nonprofit while still speaking, modeling, and going to school full-time. I did it all the only way I knew how, taking one day at a time. I learned so much as our goals and plans crystalized, and the organization took shape. I believed in my mission and disciplined myself to stay focused. And that self-discipline became the secret to my success. I tried to channel the drive of high school Desange, who was so self-disciplined, and apply her will to not just my academics but also to my personal goals.

That required me to take a new approach. I am someone who always plans everything out. Since a very young age, I have always known what I wanted. Even when I sometimes could not decide what I wanted to eat, I knew my dream: education. But with COVID, I had to adapt and go with the flow more. In many ways, the world stopped for a little while, and I learned to be okay with that and remind myself that I was at the beginning of a process of finding myself and growing.

I let God do more of the planning, which was a big exercise of trust on my part since at that time my relationship with God was really distant. For too many years my relationship with God had been dictated by Tibasima—the church I attended, when I fasted—if I didn't follow her choices about God, she would beat me. But I wanted to establish my own relationship with God.

Forging my path was very hard, partly because it meant change. Change is something that both frightens and thrills people, something that we perceive as a blessing and a need. Change helps us to develop and spurs us to act. When fueled by hope and bravery, change can make anything possible. But change can also mean leaving a part of yourself behind. For me, I had to decide which norms of the culture I was raised in were going to be part of my future.

There are things about my culture I love—how welcoming and accepting most people are, and how orphans of any age are embraced by extended family. I love that even though families aren't perfect, they hold each other close. And I think I already mentioned that our dancing and food can't be outdone.

But some parts of that culture did not fit me. Some were little things, like women not being able to wear pants (I know how to rock a pantsuit, thank you!) and having to choose modest clothing. I did not like that children could never express a differing opinion to adults for fear of being accused of talking back. And that as a child, when an adult beat me, I was supposed to just quietly take it.

But the biggest cultural barrier holding me back was the expectation that women should not express themselves—we are supposed to sit in the corner and be quiet—and I intended to make my way in the world by using my voice and speaking my mind.

I needed to figure out who I was, this child of one culture wanting to hold on to the good from it and break free of what felt wrong. Culture clashes did happen. But I tried to stay positive and understand that I needed to see things from both sides and evaluate their merits, then decide what was right for me.

During the summer of 2021, I was honored to watch my sister Zawadi graduate university. Watching her receive her degree was amazing, since none of us had been sure we'd be able to make that accomplishment happen. I was so proud—I started dancing in the morning before her graduation. I was more excited than she was!

And that night, after dinner, Tusiime, Zawadi, and I kept the dancing going, right there in the restaurant parking lot.

That summer I took classes online and planned a trip to Uganda to put my in-country unDEfeated team together. My mentors and close friends stood by me and sponsored that trip. But one week before I was to leave, Uganda went into lockdown. I changed my ticket, hoping I would be able to go in July, but Uganda was in lockdown until August. By then, school was starting for me, so I had to wait until 2022 to go.

That summer brought more educational achievements to our family. Badulu earned a bachelor's degree.

As much as there was to celebrate, it was an especially hard time for me. The emotional work I'd started the year before overwhelmed me like a flood. I had a lot of breakdowns; it was a mess. I felt alone, even when Zawadi came to stay with me. I decided I was done with riding a rollercoaster of intense emotions. It was time to let myself fall completely, so that I could get back up and fully rise.

I quit work, speaking, and modeling, and only focused on class and my self-care. I realized how much I was holding inside. I'd never before allowed myself not to be busy, to take a break and give myself the care I needed. And I found my own way to be closer to God.

Alone, I visited my trauma from my childhood. I relived all the things I'd been afraid to think about or feel, because I knew now was the time to let them go. I just wanted the pain to go away. I wanted to look back and say, I am healed. I was scared. But I was proud of the fact that I was doing the work. Then, slowly, I started being open with my close friends and talking about my trauma.

I realized I had so much anger, and it was time to let go. If I was going to start a new chapter in life, I needed to make sure I was not living in the past or living in fear. It was hurting me to hold on to the anger, and it was time to learn how to forgive, but forgiveness is not something that comes easily for me. I took the first step by forgiving myself and allowing myself to be a human being. Easy to say, but very hard to sincerely do!

I took the summer to learn and heal, to understand my past and let it be my motivation to keep going instead of letting it hold me back. I am still in the process of healing, and I do not know when I will be able to call myself completely healed.

The 2021–2022 school year was my last year of college—I graduated early with a double major in health, society, and policy and criminology and a minor in entrepreneurship and pre-business. Time will show me what is in store for me next. But right now, at this moment, I am healthy and happy.

22

UNDEFEATED

WE ALL GO THROUGH MANY ROADS IN LIFE. We all experience emotional pain sooner or later and will need to discover ways we can heal. I have so much to share with the world. If my story can help anyone find their own path out of pain and toward healing, I'll consider that a tremendous blessing. Here's what I learned about how to make it through.

Faith, while not steady in my life, did help me through. In tough times, I would remind myself that everything in life occurs for a reason. My troubles weren't unplanned. They were the fire I had to walk through to be fit to do extraordinary things.

I've learned what not to worry about. If someone did not like me, that was their problem, not mine. If they felt sorry for me, that was their problem, too, because my painful experiences have built me into the person I am today and have prepared me for this life. I could not have asked for a better path.

I've learned not to expect too much from people. Too many of us place unimaginable expectations on others or ourselves. But that's a dangerous bet. Don't assume someone else's reality can keep pace with your own imagination.

Life, I've come to learn, feels so much better when you try to make the most of your circumstances and you surround yourself with positive, like-minded people. It can sometimes be very hard to keep a positive mindset, especially when faced with tough situations. But I try to make a conscious decision daily to look on the brighter side of things. I strongly believe that what you put into life is what you will get out of it.

We develop a variety of relationships with different types of individuals throughout our lives. Our family, friends, coworkers, and loved ones may provide us with love and support. It's wonderful to have friends with whom we can chat, confide, and even share common sentiments throughout our lives, but we must keep in mind that not every relationship is positive. In order to learn, develop, and mature, we sometimes need to endure falling apart to find the people that are truly good for us. We may feel bereft or injured, yet learning from our experiences is an important element of how we navigate life.

It's undoubtedly the most difficult to let go of our loved ones. We meet a beautiful person with whom we share our entire lives, and it never occurred to us that we might split up with them one day. Even if we believe it will last forever, things may change, and saving that relationship, despite what we read in relationship magazines, can take a long time and a lot of effort. And if that relationship can't be saved, we can see it as a chance to become self-sufficient and find ourselves and the people that we are truly meant to be with.

Emotional energy isn't something we're born with, it is something we build while coping with unique events. Going through hardships builds resilience. When I discover myself in a painful and weakened place, I remind myself to hold on tight. Some wounds take greater time to heal than others.

All of us are reduced to rubble sometimes, whether by lashing out at a friend, hurting ourselves with our conduct, or cutting corners. Mistakes frequently come with overwhelming emotions of guilt, shame, self-condemnation, and humiliation. Too frequently we punish ourselves for past mistakes, as though we could in some way make up for them. We feel less-than; we call ourselves losers. We stay chained to our past, protecting ourselves from hurts and grudges, while our painful emotions gnaw away at our joy and pleasure in life.

We harm our futures when we hold onto the past. It's challenging to let go of the memories and events that had an impact on us. Whether it is a relationship, a shift in existing circumstances, or simply something that isn't always serving us well, we need to examine them, then let go in order to recover.

For a long time, I struggled with a lack of self-awareness. Self-discovery may take various forms. It includes determining your life's purpose (we all have one), as well as delving into your upbringing and disclosing the circumstances—both good and terrible—that molded you, to help you become aware of your views and actions.

What I do know is that I have been quite hard on myself for most of my life. I have not been honest with myself and have thus set myself up for disappointment by having unreasonable expectations. But in order to comfort ourselves, we lie to ourselves a lot and even cover up our own falsehoods by accepting them as truth.

What I do know is that being honest with myself and admitting and accepting my feelings has helped me overcome a lot of dread. It has helped me overcome my fears of not being good enough and not living up to the standards I set for myself. What I do know is that we are often our own worst enemies. In so many ways, we keep ourselves back, and I'm eager to break free from that habit. I'm not saying that these worries don't exist in me—they do—and I don't think they'll ever go away, but they no longer have a stranglehold on my life now that I'm aware of my genuine sentiments and beliefs. Instead, I've figured out how they can and can't impact me.

Forgiving a person is hard. But forgiveness isn't simply necessary in our everyday lives; it's critical to a healthy existence and healthy relationships. Whether or not you are trying to forgive someone who personally harms you or are seeking to forgive yourself for something you've been carrying, forgiveness is one of the toughest things to learn in life.

Luckily, I've had many wonderful people in my life to learn from. People that gave me time, financial and emotional support, patience, and a pathway to education. Those that want to help others are a gift; they change people's lives. But learning to help the right way can amplify that gift.

I wish the people that wanted to help me all saw me as a unique individual with my own background, culture, needs, preferences, and dreams. I wish people had talked to me about what they thought was best for me before making decisions, to see if I had a different opinion. I wish people had asked me what help I needed, instead of telling me how they wanted to help me.

Specifically, if you want to help a refugee, try to put yourself in that person's shoes. A good heart and empathy are important, but possibly more important is to have a desire to truly understand that person. Don't limit your knowledge about the refugee to the words on the page in their file from an agency. That information is limited, gathered for a specific purpose and likely at a stressful time, and you won't know how well the information was translated. We don't need pity, we need information. Sometimes, we just need a friend to help us navigate the system. If you choose to invite a refugee into your home, especially if you don't speak the same language, do some reliable research about their culture and background to jump-start your understanding of them. I would have loved it if my families had known the types of food I was used to and either how to braid a Black girl's hair or what hairdressers to take me to.

Through all my struggles, I felt blessed. God sent to me the people I needed at the right moments. I have not always felt loved through it all, but I kept hope and trusted that God would come through.

They say it takes a village to elevate someone, and I was fortunate enough to have more than simply the average village to elevate me. I had family that evolved as people showed me they cared. Family isn't necessarily defined by blood. Family are the people in your life who want you to be a part of their lives and who accept you as you are. The people who would go to any length to make you happy. My village, my family, were siblings, relatives, friends, and kind people along the way who had the chance to help.

. . .

I am proud to be the executive director of unDEfeated. Through our work, we amplify women's voices and fight for women and children who can't fight for themselves.

Our mission is to provide education for underprivileged youth and women with extreme financial hardship in Uganda to further their educational endeavors, provide shelter for families, and support single mothers in operating their own businesses to support their families. We believe that by investing in women, we are investing in everyone and by investing in youth, we are investing in the future.

We currently focus our work in the Ntoroko, one of the poorest districts of Uganda, located in the western region. There are many reasons for this. Mainly, cultural beliefs are forcing teenage girls out of school, which has caused a high rate of school dropouts. It's common among the Batuku and Bakonzo, the two major tribes in the district, to marry off girls at an early age, usually between thirteen to sixteen. Instead of being given opportunities for educational advancement, some of the girls are denied education and forced to work as maids or become child brides.[9] Girls dropping out of school is common in Karugutu, Rwebisengo, and Kanara sub-counties. Head teachers at primary schools in these areas report that year after year, at least a dozen children, and some years as much as thirty-five or more, drop out before completing form seven (equivalent to the US fifth grade) because of arranged marriages.[10]

Although culture plays a big role, early marriages are also a result of extreme poverty, which makes parents marry off their daughters in exchange for a bride price. A girl may also be married off early if she gets pregnant before marriage, as otherwise she is seen as a disgrace to her family and society.

Through our efforts in encouraging healthy behaviors and educational advancement, unDEfeated wants to give youth and women a voice and a second chance to find themselves.

Our work focuses on engaging with local partners to educate businesses, schools, and communities on how to work together to decrease poverty. Through our workshops, we cover areas such as entrepreneurship, women's health, the importance of education, and community leadership.

More specifically, we will help alleviate the poverty circle in the Ntoroko district by providing educational training, which will include

9   Wilson Asiimwe, "Parents marry off underage girls as climate change takes on Ntoroko," *New Vision*, February 23, 2022, https://www.newvision.co.ug/articledetails/127757.

10   "How Sexual Violence, Early Marriage Ruin Girls' Education in Ntoroko," *Charity Heart* (blog), October 6, 2018, https://platformfortheneedy.org/2018/10/06/how-sexual-violence-early-marriage-ruin-girls-education-in-ntoroko/.

entrepreneurship, financial literacy, leadership, and other business workshops to train women and youth to start and operate their own businesses to provide a sustainable standard of living to their families.

We will also decrease the illiteracy rates in the Ntoroko district by providing scholarships, mentorships, and personal development training to youth from preschool through college to educate them about the impact of early child marriage and help them pursue their careers, goals, and aspirations.

Reflecting on the many people who had been there for me, who had loved me unconditionally, who had believed in me, who had supported me, and who had showed me life is worth living, I could see my purpose. I grew up with almost no resources but so much potential that these people nurtured. They saw me and gave me my voice when I was destined not to have one. I want to support other women with their goals. I want more women to gain their voice. I want us all to speak and to live unDEfeated.

Spreading the word about the mission of unDEfeated.
Photography credit: Mwamini Ramazani

This is me about two months after we arrived in America. We had just come home from church, where I liked to wear my African traditional clothing sometimes. What I like about this picture is that look of determination on my face, which was always there.

This is me in spring 2022. I earned that smile and my joy. I can't wait to bring happiness to more women with unDEfeated.

Photography credit: Courtney Gracie

Hairstyle credit: Belvia Noudjougoto of Styles by Belvia

FOR TIBASIMA

And I want to thank you.
Thank you for being so hard on me,
I learned how to be strong.
Thank you for your slicing words,
I watched myself heal as the wounds closed.
Thank you for your ferocious challenges,
I became a character who should overcome anything.
Thank you for dragging me into the valley,
My personality used to be solid extra deeply there.
Thank you for making an attempt to break me,
I realized that I am unbreakable.
Thank you for getting beneath my skin,
The stress helped me see where I wanted to grow.
Thank you for all the confusion you brought,
It inspired me to seek the truth.
Thank you for all your messiness,
I bought smoothies when I stopped cleaning up yours.
Thank you for all your false accusations,
I got to comprehend my real self at the core.

Thank you for pressuring me to open up,
I used it as a probability to be vulnerable.
Thank you for your jarring strength,
You taught me that I could stand up to you.
Thank you for usually getting in my space,
I learned how I show up when people get too close.
Thank you for declaring what I couldn't see,
It allowed me to see the deep interior myself.
Thank you for giving up on me,
I realized in no way I was going to give up on myself.
Thank you for opening up your heart,
You unlocked my heart even more.
Thank you for making me see matters differently,
You taught me extra than I could've ever imagined.
Thank you for not loving me the best you could,
Instead of resenting you, I see it as a gift.

Thank you for all you have done for me. Growing up in your hands, I have been blessed. Even if we did not see eye to eye, you played a big part in showing me what is wrong and right. But above everything else you showed me what kind of woman I did not want to become. Thank you.

ACKNOWLEDGMENTS

AS YOU CAN SEE, I HAVE NOT WALKED ALONE; I had so many people hold my hand and help me to get where I am today. We all need someone to hold our hand to get through life. Thank you for being part of my life journey. It's easy to take the important people in your life for granted, and I want to make sure that I don't do that with you all.

To my teachers and my professors, thank you. I won't forget a single phrase that you said within the classroom. I will also not forget everything you said outside of it.

Amy and Scott Harmer, thank you so much for supporting my family. Thank you for everything you do for the refugee community. We are grateful.

Kristin and Jeremy Andrus, I don't even know where to begin. Thank you for always being willing to support my crazy ideas and come up with ways to make them work. Thank you for all the community work you do and how much you have changed lives.

Reverend France Davis at Calvary Baptist Church, thank you for being a father to my family and me. Thank you for welcoming us to the Calvary and making us feel at home. Thank you for listening. To my Calvary family, thank you for the love and support you have shown my family and me these past years.

To the First Ascent Program, board members, sponsors, and mentors, thank you for all you do. Without this scholarship, college education would not have been for me. Thank you for giving me a chance to get a higher education.

Ellen and Leon Brady, thank you for always looking out for me and my siblings. Thank you for accepting us as your own. It feels so good to know you have someone who has your back.

Beth Noymer Levine, thank you so much for helping me with publishing this book. Thank you for everything you have done for me.

One Refugee Scholarship, I am grateful. You have been there for me since the day I started my college journey while still in high school. Thank you so much; my early college experience could not have been possible without you.

ABOUT THE AUTHOR

DESANGE KUENIHIRA is the CEO and founder of unDEfeated, a nonprofit organization that provides education for underprivileged youth and women with extreme financial hardship in Uganda. The foundation supports single mothers and youth in developing entrepreneurial skills so that they can start successful businesses to support their families.

Originally from Democratic Republic of Congo, Desange lived in Uganda for twelve years as a refugee before moving to the US and becoming a US citizen. Desange holds a Bachelor of Science in criminology and a Bachelor of Science in health, society, and policy, with a minor in entrepreneurship and pre-business from the University of Utah.

Desange was named Miss Democratic Republic of Congo in the 2019 Miss Africa Utah pageant and Miss Juneteenth in 2018 and continues to represent her home country in speeches and community activities.

She was honored to be recognized for her commitment to the refugee community by being nominated for the Emerging Youth Leader Award in 2019.